Teaching Reading and Writing

A Guidebook for Tutoring and Remediating Students

Andrew P. Johnson

Rowman and Littlefield Education
Lanham • New York • Toronto • Plymouth, UK

JUN 10
JUN 10
10

Published in the United States of America
by Rowman & Littlefield Education
A Division of Rowman & Littlefield Publishers, Inc.
A wholly owned subsidary of The Rowman & Littlefield Publishing Group, Inc.
4501 Forbes Boulevard, Suite 200, Lanham, Maryland 20706
www.rowmaneducation.com

Estover Road
Plymouth PL6 7PY
United Kingdom

British Library Cataloguing in Publication Information Available

Library of Congress Cataloging-in-Publication Data

Johnson, Andrew P. (Andrew Paul)
  Teaching reading and writing : a guidebook for tutoring and remediating students /
Andrew P. Johnson.
    p. cm.
  ISBN-13: 978-1-57886-842-1 (cloth : alk. paper)
  ISBN-10: 1-57886-842-4 (cloth : alk. paper)
  ISBN-13: 978-1-57886-843-8 (pbk. : alk. paper)
  ISBN-10: 1-57886-843-2 (pbk. : alk. paper)
  ISBN-13: 978-1-57886-886-5 (electronic)
  ISBN-10: 1-57886-886-6 (electronic)
  1. Language arts. 2. Language arts—Remedial teaching. I. Title.
  LB1576.J586 2008
  428.0071—dc22   2008017721

∞™ The paper used in this publication meets the minimum requirements of American
National Standard for Information Sciences—Permanence of Paper for Printed Library
Materials, ANSI/NISO Z39.48-1992.
Manufactured in the United States of America.

This book is dedicated to
Mr. Patrick Norris of north Mankato, Minnesota.

CONTENTS

CONTENTS

PART THREE
INFORMATION AND STRATEGIES FOR TUTORING
AND TEACHING WRITING 177

LIST OF FIGURES

PREFACE

This book is designed for teachers, tutors, parents, and paraprofessionals who want to help students develop their ability to read and write. This can be done without having to buy the fancy, expensive programs that for-profit publishing companies insist are the key to success. All you need are the very simple, research-based strategies described in this book, plus paper, pencils, and a lot of good books to read. The activities here can be done individually, in small group, and with a little imagination, with a large group. If you are looking to spend a lot of money and get little in return, this is not the product for you. However, if you're looking for some simple, effective, research-based strategies to use for teaching reading and writing, this is the book for you.

Be Wary of "Research" That Isn't

In this book I describe a variety of strategies and techniques. Keep in mind, however, that there is no single solution. Although some for-profit companies who market educational products will often lead you to believe there is only one answer for children who have reading problems (and the answer is invariably their answer), they're wrong. They may even have some "research" that claims to show that their product is the best possible answer for your problem. Don't believe them for two reasons:

First, research isn't research unless and until it's subjected to peer review. Real researchers describe their research and send their research reports to a peer-reviewed journal for publication. To be accepted by a journal, the research must first pass muster by a jury of one's peers. This jury analyzes the study, looking to see if it has sound theoretical basis, if the data is correctly interpreted, or if there are any design flaws, statistical misinterpretations, or other types of errors. It is only when a study has been reviewed and accepted by a jury of one's peers that it can be called research. Until then it's simply something interesting to talk about. This is in contrast with for-profit companies, political or religious think tanks, or government agencies that make unsupported claims and call it "research." The claims they make should always be taken with many grains of salt. They often have an agenda. This means they start with the answer and look only for data that supports their answer.

Second, there is no such thing as a silver bullet, a magic potion, or a single solution to the problem of helping children who are having problems learning to read. There is no such thing as a "best method." Instead, there are many good methods. There are a variety of solutions, some of which work better for some students, and some of which work better for others. This brings up another important point: There is also no such thing as a standardized child. Each child and teaching situation is unique. Good literacy teachers have many different instructional tools in their toolbox. They use these different tools to find the combination that works best with individual students. Having many tools is better than having one tool.

Not a Buddhist Koan

Reading instruction is *not* a Buddhist koan. A Buddhist koan is a riddle without a logical answer, such as *"What is the sound of one hand clapping?"* The goal of the koan is to short-circuit the logical thinking process so that one might access higher levels of thinking and perception that may be beyond the simplistic cause-and-effect used in most of our ordinary lives.

Traditionally, schools have tried to get low-level readers to catch up to their classmates by slowing down instruction. While this may be the basis for a great Buddhist koan, it makes a pretty poor model for literacy instruction. It's impossible to catch up by slowing down. This is like saying we're going to turn right by turning left, we're going to get clean by getting dirty, or we're going to eat less by eating more. This slowed-down version of instruction results in students reading fewer books, thus being exposed to fewer concepts and words. Instead of less instruction at a slower rate, low ability readers need different types of instruction at varying rates. Low ability readers still need to encounter and interact with new concepts and vocabulary words, and they need to have high-level discussions with their peers.

Final Word

No single strategy described in this book is going to "cure" or "fix" a child who is struggling with literacy. However, all of them applied to different degrees and in different ways will work. Which strategies should you use? Use the ones that seem to work. How should you use them? Adopt and adapt. Use them in the way that seems most effective. Make them your own.

Andrew P. Johnson, Ph.D.
Center for Literacy and Inclusion
313 Armstrong Hall
Minnesota State Universiy, Mankato
Mankato, MN 56001
February 9, 2008

Note: I've included four very short chapters in the beginning of this book that explain what I'm doing in a general sense and why I'm doing it. This background information may be of use to you, but if you want to get right to the "how-to" stuff, skip to chapter 5.

PART ONE
BACKGROUND INFORMATION ABOUT READING

CHAPTER ONE
DEFINING READING

Being a good teacher of reading starts with an understanding of what reading is. What exactly happens between text, brain, and eye when we engage in this delightful, magical practice called reading?

Reading is the practice of using text to create meaning. The two key words here are creating and meaning. If there is no meaning being created, there is no reading taking place. For example, let's say that Billy encountered the following bit of text:

Bixto brum sammpo et meyo gamma. Burpo blaft darf.

Billy could certainly examine the arrangement of letter groupings and make the appropriate sounds for each, but unless he is psychotic, these would be a meaningless series of squeaks and grunts, and, as such, he would *not* be reading. Therefore we can assume that sounding out words or simply barking sounds into the air like a trained seal is not necessarily reading.

However, if I gave Billy a Superman comic strip with all the dialogue removed he would be able to look at the pictures and get some sense of what's going on. In this case, Billy is using a text (a picture text), and he is creating meaning. Thus we can say with all confidence that Billy is indeed reading. This means then that every child can read the first day of kindergarten. That is, every child can pick up a picture book and tell you what it's about. While young children may rely more on picture cues and letter cues, this will gradually change as they experience more print and get small bits of instruction along the way.

3

Reading is a constantly developing skill.   Like any skill, we get better at reading by practicing. And conversely, if we do not practice, we will not get better and our skills may deteriorate. From age three to one hundred and three, reading practice is what helps us become better readers. At age fifty, I am a better reader this year than I was last year because I have read thousands of more words and have been exposed to hundreds of new concepts and ideas. This influx of words and concepts has enhanced the processing that takes place as my eyeballs encounter text and my brain tries to make sense of it. I am just a microsecond or two quicker and more efficient than last year. Next year, at age fifty-one, I hope to be an even better reader.

Reading integrates visual and nonvisual information.   During the act of reading, the visual information found on the page combines with the nonvisual information contained in your head to create meaning. In that way, what's in your head is just as important as what's on the page in the process of creating meaning (reading).

To illustrate: One day, because I had nothing better to do, I decided to read Stephen Hawking's *A Brief History of Time: From Big Bang to Black Holes* (1988). (This tells you how boring my life has become since I started writing college textbooks.) Once I began reading I discovered that even though my eyeballs hit every word, I had very little idea about what I was reading. This was because the file folder in my head (cognitive scientists call this a schema) related to physics contains very little information. Schemata (plural form of schema) are the organized packages of knowledge your brain uses to arrange and group similar experiences and concepts. Schemata are the files in your file cabinet. Because of my puny, nearly empty schema related to physics, I had to read, reread, and re-reread each chapter several times. (I didn't get much out of the book although I still keep it on my shelf to impress people.)

I recently looked at the textbook *Literacy: Helping Children Construct Meaning* (Cooper & Kiger, 2006). Here I was able to skim it rather quickly, comprehend all of it, and remember a great deal of what I read. The same brain was used to read both texts. The difference was that this brain has a great deal of stuff floating around inside related to reading instruction and very little in it related to physics and cosmogony.

Reading is the act of linking one idea to another.   Putting ideas together to create a sensible whole is the essential part of reading. It is not necessary to know every word in order to read. Stop for a minute: As you read the last paragraph, I would wager that 99 percent of you didn't know the meaning of the word *cosmogony*. I would posit further that 98.5 percent of you kept reading anyway with absolutely no inclination to look the word up in a dictionary. You kept going because, even though you didn't know the exact definition of the word, you were still creating meaning with this text (hopefully). One idea was being linked to another, and thus, there was no need to stop. Also, you mostly likely got a general sense of the word by seeing it in the context of the sentence and paragraph. You may also have recognized a part of the word, *cosmo*, and linked it to related words that you know such as cosmos or cosmic (this is called word analysis, analogies, or looking for word families). You may have guessed that this word has something to do with space, universes, and physics (and it does).

Stopping to sound out this word or looking it up in a dictionary would have disrupted the meaning-making, idea-linking process and made comprehension more difficult. Thus, it is not always important that readers know the meaning and pronunciation of every single word they read as long as they are putting ideas together to create meaning. Good readers use minimal word and letter cues. By the way, cosmogony is a subfield of cosmology that is devoted to studying the birth of the universe. This may come in handy if you're ever on a TV game show.

References

Cooper, J. D., & Kiger, N. D. (2006) *Literacy: Helping children construct meaning.* Boston: Houghton Mifflin Company.

Hawking, S. (1988) *A brief history of time.* New York: Bantam Books.

CHAPTER TWO

FOUR LANGUAGE PROCESSES WORKING TOGETHER

Reading is not an isolated process. Four language processes work together to enhance the development of each of the others: speaking, listening, reading, and writing. Listening and reading are the receptive processes (taking in information), and speaking and writing are the productive processes (giving out information). We might also include a fifth language process: thinking (language that takes place in your head).

Language Processes Reinforce Each Other

The development of individual language processes enhances the development of others.

Listening and hearing other people use language enhances children's ability to speak. Young children first learn to speak by hearing others use language for real purposes. They grow in their ability to speak as they experiment and have others respond to their initial attempts at language. As older children hear other people use words and grammar, they increase their vocabulary (the majority of words that enter our vocabulary come from hearing other people use them), and they hear different ways of expressing themselves. Words are the tools we use for reading and writing. This auditory exposure to words and language also enhances our ability to read and write.

Reading helps students become better writers. Through reading students have incidental contact with the rules of grammar. Students develop a sense for the structure of the language and grammar and increase their vocabulary.

Writing helps in developing phonic knowledge and enhances reading fluency. Young children listen for sounds as they attempt to use letters to record their ideas on paper. Writing for older children and adults exposes us to more words and sentences and enhances our ability to quickly perceive and process these when we are in a receptive mode.

All of these processes affect the way we think, just as thinking affects our ability to perform all of them. Language is a tool of thought. We think in words. Words are used to help us interact with the thoughts of others. Reading enables us to have these interactions and form our own thoughts. Writing invites us to gather and organize our thoughts in order to clearly communicate them.

Learning to Talk

The same language-learning system involved in learning how to talk and listen is involved in learning how to read and write. How do young children learn to talk? They aren't asked to work in ability groups. They don't have experiences in failure. They don't have to suffer hours of drill and practice or practice meaningless sounds before they're allowed to talk. They're not asked to talk about things that aren't important to them or a part of their lives or experiences.

Children learn to speak because, as Noam Chomsky says, they're naturally hardwired to learn the language (Chomsky, 1968). They're immersed in actual, real-life speaking experiences. Then they're encouraged to talk about things that are of interest to them. They use language for real-life purposes. ("Cookie!") We encourage and expect them to learn differently and at different rates. We respond to them instead of correct them. We encourage creativity and humor, and language is involved in social interactions. Creative teachers can apply these same characteristics to classroom learning in K–12 learning situations if allowed to do so. And here's the thing: When you tap into students' natural interests and inclination, teaching becomes *much* easier and more enjoyable.

Learning to Read and Write

Children learn to read and write in the much same way they learn to speak and listen. That is, they learn best by being immersed in authentic reading and writing situations. Children need to read real books (as well as other types of print material such as lists, song lyrics, candy bar wrappers, and so on). They also need to read books they enjoy or find interesting (this is what adults do). And just like adults, beginning readers need to be able to talk about the books they love (just like Oprah's book club) instead of just doing book reports or comprehension worksheets. (By the way, do you think you'd do much pleasure reading if you had to do a book report or comprehension worksheet afterward?)

Children learn to write by putting their ideas on paper, writing about things that they're interested in, and getting responses to their ideas from other students and teachers. As well, letting children write for real purposes and getting responses to their ideas from real human beings is the best way for them to develop their writing ability.

References

Chomsky, N. (1968). *Language and mind*. Orlando, Fla: Harcourt, Brace & World.

HOW TO TEACH READING

So how do we go about the business of teaching children to read? We don't. Instead, we create the conditions whereby children can learn to read and develop their reading skills. As I said in the last chapter, children learn to read and write in the same way that they learned to listen and speak—that is, by being immersed in the language and by having adults around who responded to them in appropriate ways. In this sense then, we would be more accurate if we called ourselves reading-condition-creators instead of reading teachers. Below are some tips to keep in mind as we create good reading conditions.

Creating the Conditions for Learning to Read

Help children fall in love with books.   Reading is a pleasurable act. When I do it, I want to do more of it. There are wonderful stories and interesting characters found in books. I can experience magic, adventure, romance, moral dilemmas, comedy, tragedy, triumph, failure, or success. I can learn about interesting things, zip back and forth through time, and travel to the farthest reaches of the galaxy. A teacher's or tutor's number one job is to help students fall in love with books.

Create a space every day for sustained, silent reading.   Just like learning to play a musical instrument, children who are learning to read get better at it by practicing. For example, after a few piano lessons Billy would know which squiggly little mark on the paper corresponded with the correct black or white key on the piano. However, if he never practiced, he would never get beyond the stage of plodding along, stumbling, and stopping. To him, the musical text would seem like a series of single notes instead of musical phrases. There would be little pleasure in playing the piano as he would never be able to play and express whole musical ideas. This is exactly what happens if we do not provide ample time for students to "practice" their reading.

I will hit you over the head with this idea many times throughout the book, but providing ten to sixty minutes of silent uninterrupted reading time is one of the best things you can do for students of all ages. Likewise, one of the surest ways to retard children's reading progress and limit their intellectual development is to deprive them of opportunities to engage in real reading experiences. Yet, in the glorious name of phonics and standardized testing, this is what often happens. Recent studies show that primary age children spend as little as ten minutes a day engaged in authentic reading experiences (Allington, 2006).

Allow children to make choices about their reading material. Choice is important in helping readers grow. Reading is more pleasurable when we are able to make choices about what we read. Most of the time adults are allowed to choose their own reading material. We can go to the library and select any book we want. At the bookstore, nobody assigns us to groups, makes us find books at a certain level, or yells at us for reading ahead. If we become enthralled with an author, we can read as many of that author's books as we want. Likewise, if we find a book to be boring or uninteresting we can also choose not to read it. Children need to be able to make the same kinds of choices about their reading material, not all the time, but much of the time. (Choice doesn't mean total choice all the time.)

Connect reading pleasure to reading practice. A simple behaviorist principle is that if we find something to be enjoyable (a positive reinforcement), we are more likely to do that thing again. If we find something to be boring, frustrating, or meaningless (an aversive conditioner), we are less likely to do that thing again. In this sense we're not so far removed from rats running around in Skinner boxes. Now, if reading is a behavior that leads to improved reading ability, wouldn't it follow that we would try to make reading instruction as pleasurable as possible?

In the same way, if the act of reading is linked to instruction that students find unpleasant or disagreeable, they will be less inclined to engage in future reading behavior. So why can't Johnny read? It's often because we give him very little time in school to actually practice reading, and we've frustrated or bored the pants off him during what is laughingly called reading instruction.

Keep your reading program simple.   In all areas, rigor is not the same as complexity. Just because a literacy program is complicated, uses a lot of big words, contains flashy graphs and pictures, has a detailed scope and sequence, includes an elaborate assessment plan, and costs a lot of money doesn't mean it is of any worth. The three most effective literacy instructional devices ever invented are very simple things: good books, paper with lines on it, and no. 2 pencils. The only other thing to add to this list is a teacher who understands children, learning, and literacy.

Keep instruction simple.   Good teachers make things seem as simple as possible. In this way they are like gymnasts. Gymnasts are able to perform complicated moves and make them look simple. Circus performers make simple moves look difficult. As teachers we want to be gymnasts, not circus performers.

Make reading like real life.   The kind of reading and writing we have children do in school should be very much like the kind that adults do in real-life situations. In my adult life I read for pleasure or to understand ideas and information. I write to organize my thoughts, to express ideas, and to convey important information to others. I have never had to separate words into syllables; identify plot, conflict, and resolution in a story; describe an author's purpose; identify diphthongs, diagraphs, initial clusters, medial clusters, and schwa sounds; identify CVC (consonant-vowel-consonant) letter patterns; or find topic sentences in paragraphs. (By the way, if you examine paragraphs in newspapers, magazines, and books you'll find that most of them don't have topic sentences.)

I have found no research to indicate that having children do these things improves their ability to read and process text or to express their ideas on paper. So why do we continue to spend precious time in our classrooms doing these things? For the same reason we do much of what we do in education: because it has always been done that way. It's not that some of these activities may not have value; rather, they should be put in perspective or kept to a minimum.

Include talk and other forms of social interaction. Talking and social interaction enhances learning of any kind (Kauchak & Eggen, 1998). Children need to talk to each other about what they're reading and share their ideas and insights with others. In this way, the stories come to life, students gain insight and ideas from others, and language learning is enhanced.

Putting It Together

To keep children moving along the path toward becoming mature readers and writers is a fairly simple thing: We only need to provide them with large chunks of time to read enjoyable books, invite them to write about their ideas, and encourage them to share their insight and ideas with other students. Small bits of instruction should then be provided along the way. As teachers, we need to do more listening and looking, and less talking and testing.

The Dog Whisperer

I want to present an analogy that might help you to understand how children best learn literacy. On the National Geographic channel there is a program called *Dog Whisperer* with Cesar Millan. As I was watching this program I realized that this perfectly illustrates humanistic learning theory, upon which this book is based. Instead of training dogs using rewards (doggy treats) and punishment ("*bad dog*"), or other forms of external manipulation, Cesar Millan has come to understand dogs in terms of their natural behavior. That is, he understands and explains dogs in relation to their natural pack instinct, how they react to the pack leader, and their other instinctive behaviors. He uses this to teach them compatible or desired behaviors. Keep in mind, the domestication of dogs is a relatively recent event. Dogs have lived in the wild for millions of years. They have lived with humans for only a few thousand years.

In the same way, the "education" of children is a relatively recent event. The factory model that is now used to manipulate and coerce children to do our educational tricks has only been in place for a little over a hundred years. Before that, young children played, imagined, and imitated adults as a way to explore and discover their worlds and to develop the knowledge and skills that would eventually enable them to learn and survive in the adult world. (Yes, play is a natural way of learning.) Humanistic learning theory seeks to design educational experience around students' natural desires and ways of coming to know the world. (Young children need to play and experiment. Older children need to interact and explore their roles within social groups. Adolescents need to push the boundaries, discover their identities, rebel against adult authority, and try on a variety of roles and philosophies.) A humanistic curriculum would design learning experiences, not to suppress these natural ways of being, but rather to coincide with them. That is, it would use students' natural inclinations to enhance teaching and learning.

The instructional strategies described in this book are designed to complement children's natural acquisition and use of language. That is why we look for authentic reading and writing experiences, and focus on reading and writing in the context of creating meaning with print, as opposed to learning a series of subskills. Whole language seeks to keep language as whole as possible, not broken into tiny little abstract bits.

References

Allington, R. (2006) *What really matters for struggling readers: Designing research-based programs* (second ed.). Boston: Allyn and Bacon.

Kauchak, D., & Eggen, P. (1998) *Learning and teaching: Research-based methods* (third ed.). Needham Heights, Mass.: Allyn and Bacon.

A BALANCED READING PROGRAM

Reading programs need to be balanced (Cunningham & Allington, 2007). This means that it's not all just one thing (like all phonics instruction, or all reading, or all writing, or all anything). Instead, there's a little bit of this and a little bit of that. You may not have noticed, but children are not standardized products. Children learn differently, in different ways, and at different rates. Thus, in learning to read, some children need a little more of one thing while others need a bit more of another thing. Trying to push all children through the same reading program will result in the slowed growth of some and the frustration of others. This practice is called teaching the program and not children. Effective teachers teach children. Factory workers teach the program. Whenever possible, strive to be a teacher, not a factory worker.

What Does a Balanced Program Look Like?

A balanced reading program has the following characteristics.

The number one priority is to help children fall in love with books. After this, reading instruction is easy.

Conditions are created to enable students to learn to read. We don't teach children to read as much as we create the conditions whereby they can learn to read. Some children learn to read in spite of what we do to them. Instead of calling it reading class, why don't you call it reading practice? Remember, reading is creating meaning with print. It is *not* sounding out letters. It is *not* pronouncing words (see below).

You teach multiple ways to recognize words. Remember, phonics is just one of six ways to recognize words. And it is the least efficient in terms of thinking space used. These six word recognition strategies are

- **Context clues**. Figuring out what the word is by looking at what makes sense in the sentence.

- **PSR/morphemic analysis**. Figuring out what the word is by looking at the prefix, suffix, or root word.

- **Word analysis/word families**. Figuring out what the word is by looking at word families or parts of the word you recognize.

- **Ask a friend**. Turn to a friend and say, "What's this word?"

- **Skip the word**. If you are still creating meaning, why stop the process to figure out a word?

- **Phonics**. Using minimal letter cues in combination with context clues to figure out what the word is.

There is lots of reading practice. Would you expect to get better at playing golf without practicing? Certainly not. In the same way, all humans get better at reading by practicing it. Time set aside for silent reading is one of the best things you can do to promote and enhance reading (Cunningham & Allington, 2007). How much time should you set aside? You might start with the following generally guidelines: fifteen to thirty minutes a day in primary grades; thirty to sixty minutes in intermediate grades, forty to ninety minutes in middle school and high school. Earlier in the year, younger children might only be able to focus for ten to fifteen minutes. Once they learn that reading is something they'll do every day and that it is a pleasurable experience, they will be able to read for longer periods of time.

Children are invited to choose easy books. As adults, we don't always choose "challenging" material to read; we choose pleasurable material to read. Inviting children to sometimes read easier material reinforces the pleasurable aspects and enhances reading fluency. Children need to be able to practice reading by choosing easy books to read (Zemelman, Daniles, & Hyde, 2005).

Students are allowed to make choices about reading material. Can you imagine, as an adult, if you could only read what people assigned you to read? What would it be like if you couldn't go into a library and look for a book that interested you? Choice is one of the most powerful motivators for reading and needs to be included in any reading program (Zemelman, Daniles, & Hyde, 2005). However, this doesn't mean total choice all the time. Rather, there are three continuums of choice: First, a choice within a sample. Example: "We've got five books we're going to read this week. You can choose the one that you wish to read." Second, choice within a category. Example: "This month we're looking at historical fiction and historical nonfiction. You can select any book related to the Civil War." Third, total choice. Example: "Find a book that you would enjoy reading."

Reading practice sessions have more reading than skills work. Constance Weaver (2002) suggests the following formula for reading classes: 70 to 80 percent authentic reading, 20 to 30 percent skills work.

Authentic literacy activities are used most often—instead of contrived basal skills worksheets. There's nothing wrong with worksheets, as long as these aren't the only thing you use. If you look through a basal teacher's manual you'll notice that a lot of the worksheets have absolutely nothing to do with enjoying the story or helping students to create meaning with text. Part of your responsibility as an intelligent and creative teacher of reading is to save your students from these contrived sorts of activities. (These alternative, authentic activities and assignments comprise the majority of this book.)

Teachers are allowed (by their district and principal) to make choices about their students. There's a movement today for more top-down mandates by state and federal governments and by school districts. These entities, who do not know you or your children, want to tell you how to teach, what to teach, when to teach it, and how long to teach it.

Our schools need creative and intelligent teachers, yet these teachers are often denied the ability to use their creativity and intelligence in designing learning experiences. When teachers are allowed to make decisions related to teaching and learning, student achievement is enhanced (Sweetland & Hoy, 2002) and schools become more effective learning communities (Detert, Louis, & Schroeder, 2001). However, with freedom comes responsibility. Teachers must then be responsible for making sure they know what a body of research says is effective in relation to teaching and learning.

Seat work is not used to simply keep students busy. In the old days (and sometimes in the new days), students were given seat work to keep them busy while the teacher worked with a small group. This sort of busywork was often meaningless and had more to do with measuring students and keeping them silent (passive) than helping them enjoy good books or create meaning with text. In an effective literacy environment students spend most of their time reading, writing, and talking about literacy.

Voluntary reading is promoted. Voluntary reading is the reading children do at home or on their own when they are not required to do so. This is related to helping children fall in love with reading and to providing lots of reading practice (opportunities for sustained silent reading [SSR]). The amount (volume) of reading children do is related to fluency, comprehension, and achievement (Allington, 2006).

Round robin reading is avoided. Round robin reading is the practice of going around a circle or room and calling on children to read sections out loud. This is a silly practice that does more to discourage and humiliate nonreaders than to help them. Also, it slows down the reading process and decreases comprehension. But most important, this is not what real-life readers do. (I have yet to go into a library and see people sitting around a table taking turns reading out loud.)

"Well, how do I know the student is reading the assignment?"

Story maps, book talks, double journal entries are just some of the ways.

References

Allington, R. L. (2006) *What really matters for struggling readers: Designing research-based programs* (second ed.). Boston: Allyn and Bacon.

Cunningham, P. M., & Allington, R. L. (2007) *Classrooms that work: They can all read and write* (fourth ed.). Boston: Allyn and Bacon.

Detert, J. R., Louis, K. S., & Schroeder, R. G. (2001) A culture framework for education: Defining quality values and their impact in U.S. high schools. *School Effectiveness and School Improvement, 12,* 183–212.

Sweetland, S. R., & Hoy, W. K. (2002) School characteristics and educational outcomes: Toward an organizational model of student achievement in middle schools. *Educational Administration Quarterly, 36,* 703–29.

Weaver, C. (2002) *Reading process and practice* (third ed.). Portsmouth, N.H.: Heinemann.

Zemelman, S., Daniles, H., & Hyde, A. (2005) *Best practice: Today's standards for teaching and learning in America's schools* (third ed.). Portsmouth, N.H.: Heinemann.

PART TWO
STRATEGIES FOR TUTORING AND TEACHING READING

CHAPTER FIVE
ESTABLISH A BASELINE

L et's get down to the basics. For tutors and for classroom teachers it's helpful to have a general sense of students' reading grade level. This allows you to select reading materials that are appropriate. This chapter describes two types of strategies to use here: graded word lists and graded readers.

Graded Word Lists

Graded word lists are lists of words used to indicate the approximate grade level at which a student is reading. Common types of word lists are Dolch word lists and Fry word lists. You could buy a fancy book with a bunch of complex instructions or you could do an Internet search. I'd recommend the latter.

Graded word lists are to be read orally, and thus, can be used with only one student at a time. To use them:

1. Give students a list that is slightly below the grade level you think they may be at.

2. Students read the list out loud (see figure 5.1). You should have a duplicate of the list used to keep track of words read correctly and to note decoding errors.

3. Do nothing to the words that students recognize immediately. These are sight words or words they recognize without having

to use letter cues or needing to sound them out. Students receive one point for these words.

4. Put a ✓ mark next to the words that students must decode or sound out, or words that they read incorrectly at first but immediately fix. They receive half a point for these words.

5. Circle the words that students cannot read or that are decoded incorrectly. They receive zero points for these words.

In figure 5.1 the points shown at the bottom are used to determine the student's reading level. There are three levels:

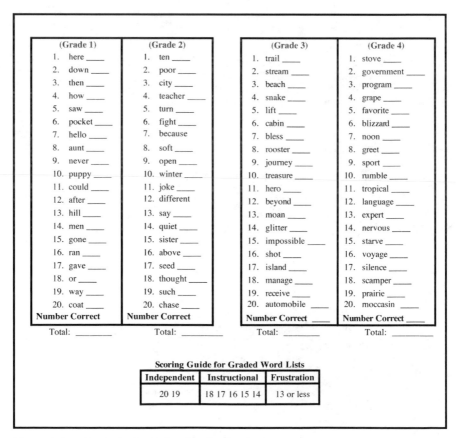

(Grade 1)	(Grade 2)	(Grade 3)	(Grade 4)
1. here ____	1. ten ____	1. trail ____	1. stove ____
2. down ____	2. poor ____	2. stream ____	2. government ____
3. then ____	3. city ____	3. beach ____	3. program ____
4. how ____	4. teacher ____	4. snake ____	4. grape ____
5. saw ____	5. turn ____	5. lift ____	5. favorite ____
6. pocket ____	6. fight ____	6. cabin ____	6. blizzard ____
7. hello ____	7. because	7. bless ____	7. noon ____
8. aunt ____	8. soft ____	8. rooster ____	8. greet ____
9. never ____	9. open ____	9. journey ____	9. sport ____
10. puppy ____	10. winter ____	10. treasure ____	10. rumble ____
11. could ____	11. joke ____	11. hero ____	11. tropical ____
12. after ____	12. different	12. beyond ____	12. language ____
13. hill ____	13. say ____	13. moan ____	13. expert ____
14. men ____	14. quiet ____	14. glitter ____	14. nervous ____
15. gone ____	15. sister ____	15. impossible ____	15. starve ____
16. ran ____	16. above ____	16. shot ____	16. voyage ____
17. gave ____	17. seed ____	17. island ____	17. silence ____
18. or ____	18. thought ____	18. manage ____	18. scamper ____
19. way ____	19. such ____	19. receive ____	19. prairie ____
20. coat ____	20. chase ____	20. automobile ____	20. moccasin ____
Number Correct	**Number Correct**	**Number Correct** ____	**Number Correct** ____
Total: _____	Total: _____	Total: _____	Total: _____

Scoring Guide for Graded Word Lists

Independent	Instructional	Frustration
20 19	18 17 16 15 14	13 or less

Figure 5.1.   Graded Word Lists for Grades 1–4

Independent level.   At this level the student can read unassisted. Students are generally able to read 98 percent or more of these words. You want to find books at this level for the student to use in pleasure reading or reading independently.

Instructional level.   At this level the student can read with some assistance. Students are generally able to read 90 to 97 percent of these words. This is the level of reading material you want to use for reading instruction. Here you will need to provide some assistance such as a story map, vocabulary help, or a story preview.

Frustration level.   At this level the student cannot be successful even with a lot of teacher help. Students are able to read less than 90 percent of these words. Avoid this level. Some people mistakenly think that challenging students will help them progress faster. Instead, you end up with frustrated learners who learn that they can't learn to read.

The websites below contain graded word lists:

www.nifl.gov/readingprofiles/SD_List_Pop.htm
www.nifl.gov/readingprofiles/resources.htm
www.webschool.wash.k12.ut.us/reading/inventory/sandiego.html
www.theteacherscafe.com/Worksheets/Reading/San-Diego-
    Quick-Printable-Reading-Assessment-Instructions.htm
www.angelfire.com/bc/capd/sight_word_lists.htm
www.theschoolbell.com/Links/Dolch/Dolch.html
www.mrsperkins.com/dolch.htm
www.kidzone.ws/dolch/grade1.htm
www.fcboe.org/schoolhp/shes/sight_words.htm
http://connwww.iu5.org/cvelem/RR/Fry_Words.html

The San Diego Quick Reading Assessment

The San Diego Quick Reading Assessment is a simpler version of the graded word list. Here, students again read the list orally. If they make one error or less, they are considered to be at their independent reading level. Two errors indicates their instructional level. Three or more errors means students are at the frustration level. Again, start a level below where you think students are. Continue until you find their independent and instructional levels.

Word Lists for the San Diego Quick Reading Assessment

Grade 1
- road
- live
- thank
- when
- bigger
- how
- always
- night
- spring
- today

Grade 2
- our
- please
- myself
- town
- early
- send
- wide
- believe
- quietly
- carefully

Grade 3
- city
- middle
- moment
- frightened
- exclaimed
- several
- lonely
- drew
- since
- straight

Grade 4
- decided
- served
- amazed
- silent
- wrecked
- improved
- certainly
- entered
- realized
- interrupted

Grade 5
- successful
- business
- develop
- considered
- discussed
- behaved
- splendid
- acquainted
- escaped
- squirming

Grade 6
- bridge
- commercial
- abolish
- trucker
- apparatus
- elementary
- comment
- necessity
- gallery
- relativity

A Word of Caution

By doing a little Internet detective work you can find many of these graded word lists. These can be used to give you a very general sense of students' reading levels. When using graded word lists it's always best to use at least two different types. Keep in mind that this is by no means an exact science. The baseline data generated from graded word lists can be used to provide you with a rough idea of where to begin. They can also be used to give you a very general sense of students' progress; however, they should never be used for program comparison or evaluation. They should also not be used to "diagnose" students or to identify students for inclusion in or exclusion from any program.

Graded Readers and Leveled Book Lists

Other methods to use in establishing a general baseline for the reading level of students are graded readers and leveled book lists. Graded readers are reading selections (books or short stories) for which the average reading grade level has been established. For example, if the reading grade level of a book is 2.0, this would be the average reading level of second-grade students.

A leveled book list provides the title of a book and the approximate grade level and month of instruction. For example, a grade level of 2.5 would mean that this book is at the average reading level of second-grade students in their fifth month of instruction. (Note: the terms *graded reader* and *level reader* are often times used synonymously.) An example of a leveled book list is included here:

Apple Bird, Brain Wildsmith—1.00
Apples, Deborah Williams—1.00
Bears, Bobbie Kalman—1.00
Big Long Animal Song, Mike Artwel—1.00
Brown Bear, Brown Bear, What Do You See? Bill Martin Jr.—1.00
100th Day Worries, Margery Cuyer—2.50
The Adventures of Granny Gatman, Granny Meadows—2.50
Cinderella Bigfoot, Mike Thaler—3.30
Class Clown, Johanna Hurwitz—3.30
Class President, Johanna Hurwitz—3.30
Clue Jr: The Case of the Chocolate Fingerprints, Parker C. Hinter—
    3.30

The websites below contain other book lists or search engines that can be used to determine the grade level of a book:

http://home.comcast.net/~ngiansante/
http://www.carolhurst.com.titles/gradetitles.html
http://www.clay.k12.fl.us/grade_level_reading_lists.htm

Also, if you work in a school that uses a basal reading program you can use the books that accompany these programs as a form of a graded reader. These books often note the approximate intended grade level. If you are tutoring apart from a school district, used basal readers can be found in many thrift stores, garage sales, and used book stores.

Using Graded Readers to Find Approximate Reading Level

Once you have a book or a sample of graded reading, use the following steps to find approximate reading grade level:

1. Select a section that contains about fifty to one hundred words (fewer for younger children, more for older children).

2. Have the student read orally (this is an individual assessment).

3. Note the words incorrectly identified by the student.

4. Determine reading level for that selection by calculating the percentage of words read correctly (divide the words read correctly by the total number of words):
   - Words correct divided by total words = reading level
   - Independent reading level = 98 to 100 percent accuracy
   - Instructional level = 90 to 97 percent accuracy
   - Frustration level = 89 percent or lower

   A score of 98 percent or higher would indicate students' independent reading level. This is the level of books that you should encourage students to read for pleasure at home and at school. A score of 90–97 percent would be their instructional level. This is the level of books that should be used for reading instruction. Reading material at the frustration level should not be used.

5. Continue with various reading samples until you can find the instructional and independent reading levels.

Fry Readability Formula and Graph

But what if you can't find reading samples that indicate a particular reading level? What can you do to figure the approximate reading level? The most widely used formula to determine grade level of reading material is the Fry Readability formula (although there are others).

To determine the grade level of a piece of reading, use the following steps:

1. Randomly select three hundred-word passages from a book or an article. Count exactly hundred words. Don't count numbers in the text, but do count proper nouns.

2. Find the number of syllables in each hundred-word selection. Figure the average number of syllables per hundred words for all three passages. (Add the three totals and divide by three.)

3. Find the number of sentences in each hundred-word selection. If the hundred-word count ends in the middle of a sentence (it most likely will), estimate the length of the sentence to the nearest tenth (1/10). (Example: 7.3 sentences per hundred words.) Figure the average number of sentences per hundred words for all three passages. Add the three totals and divide by three.

4. Look at the results of your three samples and figure the average syllable and sentence count.

5. Use the graph to find the approximate reading level (see figure 5.2).

As described above, once you find the approximate reading level, have the student read a fifty- to one-hundred-word sample. Divide the number of words pronounced correctly by the total number of words. Use the percentages described above (independent, instructional, and frustration levels) to determine the approximate reading level.

Fry Graph for Estimating Reading Grade Levels

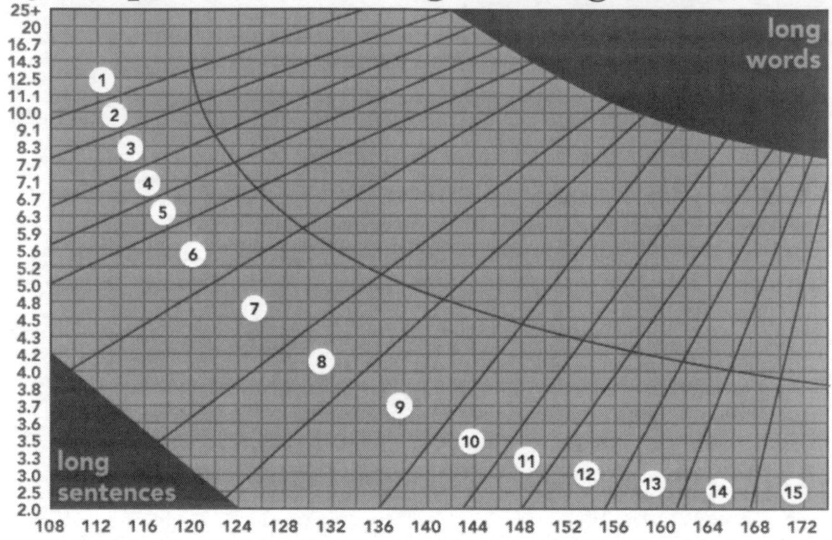

Figure 5.2. Fry Graph for Estimating Reading Grade Levels

Internet Search Terms

Graded word lists: *graded-word-lists, IFI-word-lists, Dolch-graded-word-lists, San Diego-quick-reading-assessment.*

Leveled book lists and graded readers: *reading-grade-level-online, reading-level-online, leveled-reading, leveled-reader, leveled-book-list, grade-level-reading-lists, samples-*[insert grade]*-level-reader, graded-book-lists, leveled-book-list.*

Readability formulas and graphs: *Fry-readability, Fry-readability-graph, Fry-readability-formula, readability-formula, Smog-readability-formula.*

CHAPTER SIX
DEVELOP A LOVE OF READING

A teacher's or tutor's number one job is to help children fall in love with books. Once this is done 98 percent of reading instruction is complete. However, to do this, you must have good books for them to read. What's a good book? A good book is any book that a student enjoys and wants to read. This chapter describes a few very simple ways to help children develop a love of reading.

Selecting a Book

Often, younger children will pick out a book they like, but get frustrated when they find it is too hard for them to read. Tell students that it is okay to choose a book that seems easy. We read for fun, so we want to find easy books. (How often do you select books that "challenge" you?) To see if a book is at about the right level, teach students to read the first paragraph and the last paragraph of the book. If they can read these paragraphs and they seem to make sense, then the book is at about the right level.

High/low books. High/low books are high interest/low vocabulary level books. These are good for students in fourth grade through middle school who are reading at a low grade level but don't want to be seen reading "baby books" (visit Capstone press at www.capstonepress.com/).

Comic books. Comic books and cartoons are other great sources of reading material for young, reluctant readers. With comic books, students can use the pictures to carry the story. Also, use newspaper comic strips and cartoons. Again, these are highly visual, enabling the student to use picture cues as well as word cues to read.

Graphic novels. Graphic novels are a cross between stories and comic books. They are essentially comic strips in book form or chapter books in comic strip form. Because of the visual emphasis, these can be highly motivating for some students. The websites below provide lists of comic books and graphic novels that might be used with elementary students and young adults.

Lists of recommended comic books for students of all ages:

http://ublib.buffalo.edu/libraries/units/lml/comics/pages/

Lists of graphic novels for elementary students:

http://www.ala.org/ala/booklinksbucket/graphicnovelsfory-ounger.htm
http://www.cedu.niu.edu/~fiehn/GNElemSchool.html
http://www.schoollibraryjournal.com/article/CA6312463.html
http://www.accessola2.com/superconference2006/thurs/625/best.pdf

Share Interests in Books

There are many very well-written picture books, chapter books, and young adult literature. (I'm fifty years old and I still enjoy a good picture book or young adult literature.) I would encourage you to discover this world so that you are able to share with your students what you find funny or interesting.

Share your reading interests. When appropriate, share your reading interests and experiences with students. (Of course, I'd highly recommend that you stay away from describing books on religion, politics, or ones that have sexual content. Most other topics are fair game.) Let them know the types of books you like to read. Tell them what you are reading and why you like it or don't. Let them know that it's okay not to like a book and it is perfectly acceptable to abandon it in favor of something more enjoyable. (There are so many good books in this world, why slog through something you don't enjoy?) Students need to see adult models interacting with and talking about books.

Book talks.   Book talks work best in a classroom or small tutoring group. Here a student simply stands up and tells about a book he or she has read. However, these are *not* book reports. They're also not quizzes designed to see if students have read or comprehend the book. Instead, they're just talks about books and should last anywhere from fifteen seconds to two minutes.

The two rules for book talks are that students must have read the book and they must have and hold the book while they're talking. Book talks are a simple yet highly motivating way for students to hear what others are reading. In this way, students get ideas for what they might like to read next. We do this in my graduate and undergraduate literacy classes here at Minnesota State University, Mankato. Every semester I add to my list of books to read. Over the years I have discovered countless treasures.

In your classrooms, do no more than three book talks a day. Keep a calendar of some sort for students to sign up. Make it a requirement for every student to do at least one book talk every month (or once during the quarter). If you want to make this a part of your grading system, give students full points for simply doing the book talk.

Book posters.   Just like movie posters, encourage students to create book posters for books they like.

Evaluation/critique.   This is a strategy where students evaluate a book very much like a movie critique evaluates and rates a movie (see chapter 15). Student evaluations and recommendation lists should be placed on a bulletin board or wall where everybody can see them.

Recommended book lists.   There are many organizations that publish lists of children's and young adult books that have been recommended by teachers, students, and librarians. These organizations and awards include American Library Association, International Reading Association, Newbery Medal, Michael L. Printz Award, Caldecott Medal (picture books), and Young Reader's Choice Award. Below are websites for three lists of top recommended books. The Internet search terms at the end of the chapter can also be used to find various lists of top book choices. These lists can be used to give you and your students a sense of what others have found to be good books.

International Reading Association (IRA) book choice list:

http://www.reading.org/resources/tools/choices.html

National Education Association (NEA) kids' top 100 books:

http://www.nea.org/readacross/resources/kidsbooks.html

National Education Association (NEA) teachers' top 100 books for children:

http://www.nea.org/readacross/resources/catalist.html

If you are working in a classroom or with a small group, I would encourage you to create your own top 10 (or 20) book lists. These can be compared from year to year. The conversation that takes place as children discuss the merits of each book is much more important than the actual list.

Teacher read-alouds. Read a book out loud to your students every day. This is another simple yet effective way to draw children into books. It can also be effective in helping children settle down so that they are able to concentrate after a recess or at the beginning of a reading class. The read-aloud need not be more than five to ten minutes a day. Use chapter books to enable students to follow a character or storyline over time.

Regular trips to the library. Whether as home or at school, weekly trips to the library bring children into regular contact with good books.

Create books using students' stories. As part of being a literacy teacher, you are also involving your students in the act of writing on a regular basis (see chapters 18–22). Students should be writing about their experiences. They should be expressing their thoughts, feelings, and observations. Students love to read the stories written by students their age. After these stories have been edited, collect them and create books for the classroom. You can create books by individual students, by theme or subject, or simply create random collections of students' writing. Encourage students to create pictures to accompany their stories or look for pictures from the Internet to download and paste into their stories. As well, encourage them to tell their stories by creating graphic novels or comic strips.

Language Experience Approach

The language experience approach to reading instruction helps students to make personal connections to what they read. This is because it's built directly on their personal experiences. This can be done as a class, in small groups, or individually. The steps are as follows:

1. After having an experience, ask students to tell you about the experience.

2. Capture their words on an overhead, front board (white or chalk), a computer, PowerPoint screen, or, for individual students, on a sheet of paper. For example, if I was working with an individual student, I might have that student to tell me about something that she did over the weekend. I would then write down her words (as close as possible to her telling of the story), including her idioms and slang (the computer is wonderful for this). When working with a group or a whole class, ask students for ideas about a common experience and then record them using their words. This common story becomes the basis of their reading instruction. This common story could then be used as the basis for reading practice or for choral or echo reading in order to develop fluency (see chapter 11).

Do you correct for grammar? Yes, in a very subtle and positive way. For example, if Johnny said, "*Yesterday we seen three deer in the backyard.*" You'd say, "*Yesterday I saw three deer in the backyard.*" You can also explain your grammar and punctuation as you write. Example: "*This is the end of the idea. I need to tell the reader to stop. I better put in the period to use as a stop sign.*"

3. Create books by collecting the stories and experiences of many students. Again, students love to read the stories written by students their age. You can save these stories from year to year. You can also put these stories in PowerPoint and include pictures.

Reading Attitude Surveys

You can become a better reading teacher by understanding what and how your students like to read. Do this by designing your own reading attitude survey. Use any of the questions below for your survey (include your own questions or adopt and adapt the ones below).

Interest Inventory
Always-5, Often-4, Sometimes-3, Seldom-2, Never-1

I borrow books from the library or school. ___
I read things on the Internet. ___
I read before I go to bed. ___
My parents read to me. ___
I read parts of a newspaper. ___
I enjoy reading class.___
I read magazines. ___
I read for enjoyment. ___
I read because I have to. ___
I read outside of school. ___

Open-Ended Reading Questionnaire

Reading books at home is . . .
The best book I ever read was . . .
Reading is hard when . . .
Most books are . . .
When I see a library I . . .
Reading class is . . .
I think reading . . .
When my teacher reads a book to us I . . .
I think the newspaper is . . .
My favorite magazine is . . .
Some of my favorite books are . . .

Reading Survey

• Reading is my favorite subject in school.
 Yes ___ No ___ Sometimes ___

• I usually understand what I read in books.
 Yes ___ No ___ Sometimes ___

- I have read some very enjoyable books.
  Yes ___ No ___ Sometimes ___

- I like hearing about what other students are reading.
  Yes ___ No ___ Sometimes ___

- I like to hear my teacher read stories out loud.
  Yes ___ No ___ Sometimes ___

- I like to borrow books from the library.
  Yes ___ No ___ Sometimes ___

Open-Ended Survey

In reading class I'd like to . . .
I read because . . .
The kind of book I'd really like to read would be . . .
Reading in school would be more interesting if . . .
Reading is sometimes difficult because . . .
I would like to read about . . .
I'd like to read more . . .
I'd like to read less . . .
When I read I have to . . .
Reading class is interesting when . . .
When reading, I am successful when . . .

School Attitude

School is . . .
I wish teachers would . . .
Going to school is . . .
To me, homework is . . .
When I finish high school I will . . .
When I take my report card home . . .

Reading Process

When I have to read . . .
When I read math problems . . .

I like to read when . . .
For me, studying is . . .
Reading science . . .
I'd read more if . . .
When I read out loud . . .
Reading is . . .
I cannot read when . . .
When reading new words I . . .
I read better when . . .

Reading Interests

To me, books . . .
I like to read about . . .
I'd rather read than . . .
Comic books are . . .
I like reading about . . .
I don't want to read about . . .
The best thing about reading . . .
I laugh when I read about . . .
I want to read more . . .
One of the best books I've ever read is . . .

Reading Class

In reading class I like . . .
In reading class I don't like . . .
In reading class I wish we would do more . . .
This helps me learn to read . . .
I like reading these kinds of books . . .
I like reading these kinds of things . . .

Writing/Language Arts

In our writing (language arts) class I like . . .
In our writing (language arts) class I don't like . . .
In our writing (language arts) class I wish we would do more . . .

In our writing (language arts) class I wish we would do less . . .
In our writing (language arts) class I would like to write more . . .
In our writing (language arts) class I would like to write fewer . . .

Use no more than four to six questions for an open-ended survey or ten questions for a close-response survey. Give the survey and then organize and tally the results. This will help you understand your students and design more appropriate reading experiences. You might also organize and display the results in a way that students can see and assimilate. For example, when looking at the open-ended questions, look for categories or top responses for each. And finally, students always appreciate being asked. A survey like this demonstrates to them that you are interested in their ideas and that you want to create a successful and interesting reading experience.

Internet Search Terms

High/low books: *high/low-books* or *high-low-books, high-low-readers, elementary-school-comic-books, graphic-novels, graphic-novels-elementary-school, graphic-novel-elementary-classroom.*

Recommended book lists: *IRA book-choice, Printz-book-list, Newbery-winners-list, Caldecott-winners-list, young-readers-choice-awards-lists, books-kids-choice-list.*

CONTEXT CLUES

Most mature readers use context clues to recognize unknown _____ in a sentence. (I'm sure most of you automatically filled in "words" in the blank in the previous sentence.) This is a cloze activity. It's a sentence with one word missing. For very low level readers, provide one letter clue. It could also be a paragraph with one or more words missing in each sentence. Students use the context of the sentence or paragraph to identify the missing or unknown word. (Do an Internet search using the terms at the end of this chapter. You'll find hundreds of free cloze worksheets and other context clue activities. You can also create your own cloze activities.) Here is an example of a cloze sentence:

• **At school I sit in my _____.**

or

• **At school I sit in my d____.**

Cloze Activities

Cloze activities help students learn to use context clues to identify unknown words as they read. These activities can be done individually or with groups of students. Keep it fun and relatively brief. Tell students that you're playing detective and looking for clues to figure out the missing word.

CHAPTER SEVEN

The Process

1. Find or create cloze sentences. I find it is most effective to create my own sentences that are about or directly related to students. You can also create sentences related to what students are reading or studying about. This produces a more meaningful reading experience and makes learning to read easier and more interesting.

2. Present the sentence with the word covered up (or missing) on a whiteboard or a piece of paper. If you are using a big book, chart, or paper for your sentences, cover the word with a 3x5 card and a piece of tape or sticky notes.

   • **On the way to school Johnny fell in the _____.**

3. Ask students, "*What word would make sense in this sentence?*" Write two or three of their ideas on the board or paper. It is okay to get a little silly with this. (Johnny fell in the lake. Johnny fell in the pudding. Johnny fell in the hole. Johnny fell in the ice cream.)

4. Uncover the first letter and ask, "*Do you want to change your mind?*"

5. Uncover the second letter and again ask, "*Do you want to change your mind now?*" By this time most students will have figured out the word.

6. Reread the complete sentence. Ask students if the sentence makes sense.

Remember, this should be a simple activity using one to four sentences and lasting no more than eight to ten minutes. Its purpose is to develop students' ability to use context clues. Real practice and development of this skill comes from their independent reading of books that they have chosen.

Word Box

You can vary the cloze activity by creating a paragraph with a word box:

Johnny ran upstairs to his _____ to look for his shoes. He couldn't _____ them anywhere. Next, he _____ in the closet. This is where he saw the big, horrible _____. He ran out of there as _____ as he could.

   Word Box: monster, find, looked, fast, bedroom

The benefit of the paragraph is that it provides a more authentic reading context. (Students are more apt to read paragraphs than single sentences in the real world.) Also, the student is able to use the context of the entire paragraph to help find the right word.

Maze

A maze is a sentence with two or three alternative words. The student must circle the word that makes the most sense in the sentence:

> Johnny loves to [plan-play-put] basketball. Every day after [school-scoop-skip] he goes right to the basketball [can't-coop-court].

Doing an Internet search using the term *maze* may not produce very good results; however, you will find many examples of maze activities doing a *cloze* Internet search. And like cloze sentences, you can create a more meaningful experience by designing your own sentences around students' interests and experiences. These usually result in a more powerful learning experience. Within a school setting, you can also use maze and cloze activities to reinforce words and concepts found in students' reading material or used in other curriculum areas. For example, you could design them to reinforce vocabulary and concepts from your science, social studies, health, math, or other subject area classes.

Context Clues while Reading

On those occasions when you have students read out loud, encourage them to use context clues instead of phonetic or letter cues. For example, if they get stuck on a word don't automatically say, "Sound it out." This actually makes reading harder because students must now try to hold all the letters and sounds in their limited short-term memory instead of holding a few ideas. Instead say, "What word makes sense in this sentence?"

Keep it simple. Keep it short. Keep it fun. Doing cloze activities is a means to an end (reading); it's not an end in and of itself.

Internet Search Terms

Cloze activities: *cloze, cloze-activities, cloze-worksheets, cloze-reading.*

Context clues: *context-clues, context-clues-activities, context-clues, teaching, context-clues-reading, context-clues-lessons.*

WORD ANALYSIS

Seeing Parts within a Word

While some methods of reading instruction such as direction instruction advocate teaching only one word-recognition strategy (phonics), holistic approaches to literacy teach students to use six. These strategies are presented again here.

1. **Context clues**. Figuring out what the word is by looking at what makes sense in the sentence.

2. **PSR/morphemic analysis**. Figuring out what the word is by looking at the prefix, suffix, or root word.

3. **Word analysis**. Figuring out what the word is by looking at word families or parts of the word you recognize.

4. **Ask a friend**. Turn to a friend and say, "What's this word?"

5. **Skip the word**. If you are still creating meaning, why stop the process to figure out a word?

6. **Phonics**. Using minimal letter cues in combination with context clues to figure out what the word is.

Word analysis is a skill that helps students to identify unknown words by looking for familiar word parts. For example, let's say you encountered the following sentence:

Sam's <u>metacognitive</u> skills helped him read and understand his textbooks.

Let us pretend also that you're not familiar with the word *metacognitive*. Are there any parts of this word that you do recognize? You might recognize *meta*, and *cognitive*. You can probably pronounce the word, but what does it mean? The sentence itself gives us a clue. It tells us that metacognitive skills are ones that help you comprehend textbooks. Cognition means thinking. Meta means above or about. Metacognition means thinking about thinking. In this sense, it means stopping and checking to see if you understand. Let's read the sentence to see if that makes sense.

Sam's <u>metacognitive</u> skills (stopping to check for understanding) helped him read and understand his textbooks.

Yes, it does make sense. So, we were able to use both context clues and word analysis to recognize and then figure out what that word might mean. This is the same process you should use to guide young readers if they are stuck on a word while reading:

1. Ask what word would make sense in the sentence (context clues).

2. Ask if there are parts of the word that are recognized. For example, if Johnny got stuck on the word *flip* when reading, I would ask him, "Is there any part of this word that you do recognize? Do you see any word parts or word families?" I would then help him see the *fl* beginning blend and also the *ip* word family.

3. Using the word parts to make the word.

4. Reread the sentence using the new word.

5. Check to see if it makes sense.

In the old days when children encountered a word they did not recognize we would demand that they sound it out. However, this should be our last option. Using context clues and looking for familiar word parts are both more efficient than sounding out every individual letter. These strategies enable the reader to focus on the context or on parts of the word. This frees up more space in working memory to use to construct meaning. This becomes the basis then for the next word-recognition activity: *onset-rimes* or *word building*.

Onset-Rimes

Do an Internet search using the terms for word building (see terms at the end of this chapter). You'll find many different kinds of onset-rime and word building activities that you can download. These are good sources if you know how to use them. So let me explain.

An *onset* is the beginning part of a word. It's the first letter or letter blend that you encounter. In the word *slip* the onset is *sl*. In the word *tape* the onset is *t*.

A *rime* is the word family, sometimes called phonograms. (And yes, rime is spelled correctly here.) The rime in the word *tape* is *ape*. The rime in the word *slip* is *ip*. Common word families or rimes are shown below:

ab - ack - ad - ade - ag - ake - ice - id - ide - ig - ike - ime - op - ot - ound - out - own - ub - ut - us - un - um - ug - uck - ish - it - ite - ive (hive) - ive (give) - eed

The strategies (games or activities) described in the rest of this chapter are all designed to help students develop the ability to see onsets and rimes within words. The first activity is called word building.

Word Building from Rime to Onset

Start by making posters of two or three common word families. The rime should be displayed on top of the column with all variations below. If you are working individually with a student, these posters can simply be written on pieces of paper and taped on a wall or pinned to a bulletin board where you are working. (Use 14- to 16-point type if you are making these posters on your computer.) For small groups or for use with the whole class, create larger posters that can easily be seen and read. To help reinforce these word families, have students help you create these posters (they do the writing or typing with your guidance).

<u>AT</u>	<u>IN</u>	<u>ATE</u>
hat	tin	hate
mat	bin	late
cat	kin	Kate
sat	fin	plate
fat	pin	date
flat	win	fate
spat	shin	mate

I'll take you through all the steps of a word building activity from rime to onset:

1. Show the student the rime "at" on a whiteboard or piece of paper: "This is the 'at' word family. It makes the 'at' sound. Aaaaaaa-tuh. Aaaaa-tuh, as in bat or cat. I want to change at into something that I can put on my head. What letter would I need to turn 'at' into 'hat'?"

    at

2. Make the "huh" sound until the student identifies the "h." Have him or her write the "h" in front of "at" to make the word "hat." Have him pronounce the word.

    h → at → hat

3. Right below the word "hat" write another rime "at": "Now I want to change this into something I can lay down on. What letter do I need to change to turn 'hat' into 'mat'?"

    at

4. Make the "mmmm" sound until the student identifies the "m." Ask the student to write the "m" in front of "at" and pronounce the word.

    m → at → mat

5. Continue using one or two other word families. Do no more than three rimes at any one setting.

Again, you do not need any fancy equipment or expensive programs for this. A paper and pencil or a small whiteboard will be very effective. Keep this activity simple, fun, and short (five to ten minutes at the most). Remember, our goal is not to do onset-rime activities; rather, the goal is to read and enjoy good books. Sometimes we forget this. We get so involved with our phonics drills, standardized tests, comprehension worksheets, syllable dividing, and finding CVC letter patterns that we lose sight of the big picture: Real humans read books to enjoy them or to get information from them. All instruction should reflect this purpose.

If you have the word families displayed on a wall someplace (a word wall—described below) you can extend this activity by making word family riddles. Example: "I'm thinking of a word in the 'in' family. It is something found on a fish." This is a fun and simple way to develop and reinforce students' ability to recognize parts within a word. Eventually they will want to create their own riddles for you.

Word Building from Onset to Rime

After a while, reverse the process. Start with the onset and look for the rime. I'll take you through all the steps:

1. Have a word wall or posters with several word families displayed (I'll describe word walls below). On a whiteboard or piece of paper show students the rime. Example: "This is the beginning sound 't.' What word family would I need to add to get 'tip'?" Make sure you say the two parts several times: "'tuh'...'ip.'"

   t

2. If the student is having problems identifying the "ip" family, point and read through the word families until the student hears one that makes sense to him. "Is it 'ab'? 'tuh'...'ab'? Is it 'ap'? 'tuh'...'ap'? Is it 'ip'? 'tuh'...'ip'? Yes, that's right. It is the 'ip' family." Have him write the phonogram "ip" after "tip."

   t → ab, t → ap t→ ip

   t → ip → tip

51

3. Right below "tip" write another "t." "Okay, now I want to turn this 't' into a metal, something hard. I want to make it into 'tin.' What word family would I have to add to 't' to get 'tin'?"

t

4. Continue with other onsets and other rimes. Do no more than three rimes at any setting. You can go back and forth from these, from onset to rime and back again.

t → in → tin

Onset-Rime Equations

Another game (and call it a game) is onset-rime equations where you create mathematical sentences using onsets and rimes. Use mathematical symbols (+, −, =) to add and subtract various onsets and rimes in order to form equations that create words. Start with some easy ones and get more complicated as students are ready. Eventually students will want to create their own. An example of onset-rime equations is presented here:

v + ent = ____ (vent)

vent − v = ____ (ent) + beginning t = ____ (tent) − ent = (t) + ab = ____ (tab)

A quick reminder: All these onset-rime activities are designed to help students develop the ability to see word parts within words they don't recognize. While some may be more effective than others for particular students, no single activity or strategy is best. No single activity or strategies should be used in isolation. And most important, *all strategies and activities should be used in the context of reading, enjoying, and talking about good books!*

Word Walls

As the name implies, word walls are words that are displayed on a wall (or bulletin board). More specifically, these are words on butcher paper, poster, or on a bulletin board that are somewhat permanent. The words are grouped by word family, letter pattern, or subject and can be referred to and used in a variety of ways (Cunningham & Allington, 2007). Below are some of the many different types of groupings that can be used with word walls:

1. Phonograms or word families.
<u>out</u> - about - doubt - pout - route - stout
<u>in</u> - tin - bin - kin - fin - pin - win

2. Vowel sounds.
<u>Short a</u> - hat - ant - apple
<u>Short i</u> - tin - tip - igloo
<u>Short u</u> - up - fun - us

3. Words we confuse.
their - there - they're
too - two - to

4. Words we often misspell.
separate - necessary - about - tomatoes - potato - model

5. Subject-related words.
<u>Space words</u> - rocket - asteroid - planet - universe - moon - comet - Mars - atmosphere

6. Words from a book students are reading.
<u>Harry Potter words</u> - magic - castle - wand - gown - castle - angry - friends - game - study

7. Big, interesting, or astonishing words.
compliment - plethora - accomplishment - recognize - incredible - downloading - sortie

Riddles

As described above, riddles are a short, simple way to reinforce a variety of vowel sounds, beginning sounds, and phonograms. Keep this simple and fun. For phonograms you would say something like, "I'm thinking of a word in the 'out' family that's something you do when you are mad or upset."

Sentences

Ask students to use one or more words in a category to create oral or written sentences. Examples include:

Adjective sentences. Students create funny, bizarre, strange, happy, large, small, scary, mysterious, dark, bright, bumpy, smooth, or [*insert your own adjective*] sentences with a word family on the word wall. For example, they could create (*write or say*) a funny sentence with a word in the "ate" family.

Extend the activity by asking students to create an adjective sentence using two words from a word family. Extend further by mixing and matching: Create a happy sentence using the "at" family and the "ate" family. Or create a happy sentence using the "in" family with a "short a" word. Or create a happy sentence using a word from our science unit and the "out" family.

Topic sentences. These are the same as adjective sentences, except here students create sentences about a given topic. (It works best to choose topics connected to students' lives, experiences, or other curriculum areas.) For example, your students may be enthralled with football. They like talking about it, playing it, and reading about it in the newspaper. Ask them to create football sentences using words from one or more word families. In the same way, if students are studying a unit on birds in science, have them create bird-related sentences.

Wide-open sentences. Leave the topic or adjective wide open. Ask, "Who can create an interesting or important sentence using at least one word from the 'in' family?" Or if you are working with just one student, "Can you create an interesting or important sentence using at least one 'short-i' word?" Extend as described above.

Phonogram Treasure Hunts

Treasure hunts can be used with word families, vowel sounds, letter blends, grammatical elements, or any other element or skill you wish to reinforce. Here students are asked to look for specific things using a data retrieval chart. A data retrieval chart (DRC) is any type of visual organizer that enables children to organize data as they gather it (figure 8.1). Using a book they have read or a short article, students put a tally mark in the

appropriate column every time they encounter an example of that particular element. You can extend this in three ways by

1. Asking students to make predictions: "Make a prediction. Do
   you think there'll be more 'in' words or 'ake' words in this chapter?" This gets them using a method of science (ask a question
   and then gather data to answer your question).

2. Creating bar graphs or tables to display the numerical data (see
   figure 8.1).

3. Comparing two stories or two pieces of writing using graphs
   or tables.

Using Familiar Words, Experiences, and Concepts

Using word analysis or word families is much more effective if the word is
in students' vocabularies. In this way they are encountering words they
know but don't immediately recognize.

I want to end this chapter by taking a look at the types of reading material we ask children to use to learn to read. It's much easier for children
to read if they're encountering words in text that are also in their vocabulary and if they're reading about something they know about or have experienced. If I were to ask a group of fifth-grade students to read a
sentence in which they had to recognize the word *gestalt* or *synchronicity*,
I would most likely be setting them up for failure. While some might be
able to sound them out, these words not likely to be in their listening vocabularies, and thus, are meaningless to them.

A universal truth: It's hard to create meaning when the text you are
reading is filled with meaningless words and concepts. It's much harder to
learn to create meaning with meaningless words and concepts. And if
you're not creating meaning, you're not reading.

What this means for low level readers is that the reading material we
choose to use for their reading instruction or tutoring experiences should
contain words with which they are familiar and concepts that they have
experienced. At the very least, the words they read should be within their

DATA RETRIEVAL CHARTS

Phonograms

in	at	ake

Vowel Sounds

long A	long I	long O

PHONOGRAM GRAPH

Word Family Graph

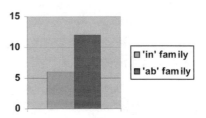

Figure 8.1. DRCs, Graphs, and Tables

Word Family Table

'in' family	12
'ab' family	6

COMPARING STORIES USING A GRAPH

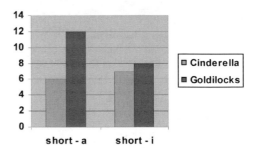

Comparing Stories Using a Table

STORY	SHORT - A	SHORT - I
Cinderella	6	7
Goldilocks	12	8

listening vocabulary. Again, this is why the Language Experience Approach described in chapter 6 can be such a powerful method to use in creating reading material for them to read and practice.

Last Word

In this chapter I have shown several strategies that can be used to develop students' ability to use word parts as a strategy to recognize unfamiliar words. Again, these are all means to the greater end, which is reading and enjoying good books. When students are reading orally and get stuck on a word, you can do the following:

1. Ask the student what word makes sense within the sentence.

2. Ask the student if he or she recognizes any parts of the word.

3. Ask the student to use the first letter of the word to give him or her a clue.

4. Ask the student to sound out the word (using phonics to unlock the word). Using phonics to parse each individual letter should be the last option.

Internet Search Terms

Word building: *onset-rime, onset-rime-activities, word-building, word-building-activities,* or *phonogram-activities.*

Word wall: *word-wall, word-wall-lists, word-wall-activities, interactive-word-wall, word-wall-lessons.*

Phonograms: *word-analysis-activities, teaching-phonograms, phonogram-games, phonogram-activities, word-families, word-family-lessons, word-family-activities.*

References

Cunningham, P. M., & Allington, R. L. (2007) *Classrooms that work: They can all read and write.* Boston: Allyn and Bacon.

MORPHEMIC ANALYSIS: PREFIXES, SUFFIXES, AND ROOT WORDS

Morphemic analysis is a fancy way of saying that you recognize unknown words by looking for familiar prefixes, suffixes, or root words (PSR) in them. You can find an abundance of activities and worksheets by conducting an Internet search using the terms at the end of this chapter. The information here will provide you with some background information about how to best use them.

Prefixes and Suffixes

Harp and Brewer (2005) suggest that formal instruction with prefixes and suffixes should begin when students are reading at the third-grade level. But this instruction should be rather limited since we don't encounter many different prefixes when we read. White and colleagues found that the four most common prefixes are used in about 65 percent of all the words used in school (White, Sowell, & Yanagihara, 1989). Likewise, the three most common suffixes appear in approximately 64 percent of all the words used in school. The lists below show the rank and approximate number of prefix and suffix words that children will encounter in their reading.

Prefix Words
un – 782
re – 401

in, im, ir, il, not – 313
dis – 216
en, em – 132
non – 126
in, im, in, or into – 105
over (too much) – 98
mis – 83
sub – 80
pre – 79
inter – 77
fore – 76
de – 71
tran – 47
super – 43
semi – 39
anti – 33
under (too little) – 25
All others – 100

Suffix Words

s, es – 673
ed – 435
ing – 303
ly – 144
er, or – 95
ion, tion, ation, ition – 76
ible, able – 33
al, ial – 30
y – 27
ness – 26
ity, ty – 23
ment – 21
ic – 18
ous, eous, ious – 18
en – 15
er (comparative) – 15
ive, ative, itive – 15

ful – 14
less – 14
est – 12
All others – 160

For teachers and tutors, it makes sense then that only the top four prefixes and the top three suffixes be the initial focus for instruction. Also, keep in mind that prefixes and suffixes are often not very reliable in terms of their meaning and spelling. For example, *reload* has a "re" prefix but *repeat* does not. *Immature* has an "im" prefix but *important* does not. Thus, prefixes and suffixes should take some, but not a great deal, of your instruction time. Most of your instructional time and practice should focus on sight words (chapter 10), context clues, word families, phonics, language experience approaches, writing, and reading good books.

Teaching about Prefixes

Explain to students that a prefix is a word part added to the front of a real word to change its meaning. The original word has to be a real word or it's not a prefix. For example, in the word *recess*, "re" is not a prefix because "cess" is not a real word by itself; however, in the word *rewind*, "re" is a prefix because *wind* is a real word by itself.

Again, the unreliability of prefixes and suffixes tells us that it's not pragmatic to spend a lot of time memorizing and drilling definitions. Instead, focus on helping students to recognize or perceive common prefixes. Here, you can treat prefixes very much like the word families described in chapter 8. Create a word wall list of words that start with the prefix "re." This list can be referred to in the context of teaching and used for a variety of activities.

Introducing new prefixes. When introducing a new prefix show students (a) the regular form of the word in the context of a sentence, (b) the new prefix by itself, and (c) the new word with the prefix attached. Then, try to define the prefix. For example:

- I was **clean**. I fell in the mud and I was not clean, or **unclean**. (**clean – unclean**)

  un + clean = unclean

- I was **happy**. Then I dropped my cake and I was not happy, or **un-happy**. (**happy – unhappy**)

  un + happy = unhappy

- To put my shoes on I had to **tie** them. To take them off I had to **un-tie** them. (**tie – untie**)

  un + tie = untie

Defining prefixes. The hardest part of teaching prefixes is defining them *using kid language.* Below are the most common prefixes along with some simple definitions and examples. Show or say both words in the context of a sentence then use lots of examples and lots of pictures.

- **un = not:** unclean, unsafe, unhappy, unable

  un = do it over, do it backwards, or do it in reverse: untie, undo, unwrap, unhook, unfasten

- **re = again or repeat:** reread, reboot, recheck

- **il, im, ir, in = not:** (il) illegal, illiterate; (im) immature, imperfect, impolite, impossible; (ir) irresponsible, irregular, irrational; (in) invisible, inexpensive, inaccurate

- **dis = not:** disable, disapprove, dishonest, disorder also, **reverse or opposite:** disassemble, disarm, disappear

Teaching about Suffixes

Suffixes should be taught in the same way as prefixes. Make sure students see the word initially without the suffix and then with the suffix. In your initial teaching of suffixes (and prefixes) try not to include or call attention to any of the spelling anomalies. Look for words (when possible) that change meaning by simply adding the prefix or suffix. Example, in looking at the "est" suffix I would not make mention of instances of changing the "y" to an "i" as in happiest.

Introducing new suffixes. Below are three examples of how you might go about introducing new suffixes:

- I have one **dog**. Maria has two **dogs**. (**dog – dogs**)

  dog + s = dogs

- Today I will **stop**. Yesterday I **stopped**. (**stop – stopped**)

  stop + ed = stopped

- I like to jump. Right now I am **jumping**. (**jump – jumping**)

  jump + ing = jumping

Defining prefixes. Below are the three most common suffixes along with some simple definitions and examples.

- **s, es = more than one:** dogs, trees, balls, clouds, dishes, glasses, boxes

  also, **is doing it right now:** runs, plays, washes, fixes, sleeps

- **ed = happened before, in the past:** washed, dropped, played, jumped

- **ing = doing it right now:** jumping, running, sleeping, playing, washing

Activities for Developing Morphemic Analysis

Many of the games and activities described in chapter 8 can be used here. Here are some variations.

Flash cards. You can play a variety of flash card games (see chapter 10) with prefix and suffix words; however, make sure the root word is already in students' reading vocabulary. This is not the place to be introducing new words. Also, when making flash cards, highlight the prefix or suffix using a different color of ink or by underlining it (colors are best). Keep in mind the goal of flash cards is to develop the ability to recognize prefix and suffix words instantly. Their use should be brief and quickly paced.

Word-O. Played like Bingo, this game works best with three or more students. Depending on the age of your students, create blank Word-O cards using 3x3, 4x4, or 5x5 squares (or let students create their own). Identify ten to fifteen words to use. Let students write the words anywhere they want on their Word-O cards (figure 9.1). They can use any word twice. Create 3x5 cards that have the identified words written on them. There should be two cards for every word. Mix up the cards. The game is played by selecting a card and reading it out loud. Then turn the

restart	skipped	started	starts
starting	replay	skipping	rewind
played	plays	play	skips
winds	winding	wind	skip

Figure 9.1.   Word-O Card

card around for students to see. They should circle the word (or put a marker on the word if you want them to use the same card twice) when it is read aloud. The person who gets four in a row in either direction first is the winner.

When I play this game, I have students create a new card every game. I identify the words and have students write them as I say them. This gets them writing and saying the words after each game.

Word walls.   Create word walls using the most common prefixes and suffixes and samples of each. Use the same word wall activities described in chapter 8.

Writing prompts.   Create open-ended, student-centered word prompts using a word that contains a prefix or suffix. Example: "I like playing . . ." or "I am unhappy when . . ."

Treasure hunts.   The treasure hunts described in chapter 8 can also be used with prefix or suffix words:

IN   RE   UN

Like before, students can create tables or graphs with the data they find. They can also compare one story to another.

Internet Search Terms

Morphemic analysis: *morphemic-analysis,   teaching-morphemic-analysis, recognizing-words-morphemes, reading-morphemic-analysis.*

Teaching prefixes and suffixes: *teaching-prefix,   teaching-suffix, prefixes-and-suffixes, teaching-prefix-suffix, prefix-suffix-activities, prefix-suffix-reading-instruction.*

References

Harp, B., & Brewer J. (2005) *The informed reading teacher: Research-based practice.* Upper Saddle River, N.J.: Pearson.

White, T. G., Sowell, J., & Yanagihara, A. (1989) Teaching elementary students to use word-part clues. *The Reading Teacher, 42*, 302–8.

SIGHT WORDS: MOST FREQUENT WORD LISTS

Recognizing Words Instantly

Sight words are words that students recognize instantly (on sight). These are words for which they do not need to use letter cues, word parts, or context clues to know what they are when encountered in a text. Fluent readers have a large sight word vocabulary while less-fluent readers have a small sight word vocabulary. Thus, part of helping less-fluent readers become more fluent involves increasing their sight word vocabulary.

But what words should students know by sight? Answer: The words that are used most frequently. A quick Internet search using the terms for sight words at the end of the chapter will provide you with various lists of words that should make up students' sight word vocabularies. As well, the websites listed below contain lists of words that are most frequently used in text.

http://www.kidzone.ws/dolch/grade1.htm
http://www.fcboe.org/schoolhp/shes/sight_words.htm
http://www.theschoolbell.com/Links/Dolch/Dolch.html
http://www.netrover.com/~jjrose/dolch/intro.html

In your Internet search you will most likely run across the websites of some very creative, savvy teachers who put important material on websites for parents. I commend these teachers as it helps parents understand what the teachers are doing in their classrooms and provides parents with material they can use at home to work with their children. It also provides ideas for other classroom teachers to use.

There are various kinds of sight word lists (Dolch, Fry, MFW, instant words, and so on). There are slight differences in these. Below is the Dolch list of basic sight words presented in order of their frequency. These are the 220 most frequent words (MFW) found in books that children read:

> **Dolch List.** the - to - and - he - a - I - you - it - of - in - was - said - his - that - she - for - on - they - but - had - at - him - with - up - all - look - is - her - there - some - out - as - be - have - go - we - am - then - little - down - do - can - could - when - did - what - so - see - not - were - get - them - like - one - this - my - would - me - will - yes - big - went - are - come - if - now - long - no - came - ask - very - an - over - yours - its - ride - into - just - blue - red - from - good - any - about - around - want - don't - how - know - right - put - too - got - take - where - every - pretty - jump - green - four - away - old - by - their - here - saw - call - after - well - think - ran - let - help - make - going - sleep - brown - yellow - five - six - walk - two - or - before - eat - again - play - who - been - may - stop - off - never - seven - eight - cold - today - fly - myself - round - tell - much - keep - give - work - first - try - new - must - start - black - white - ten - does - bring - goes - write - always - drink - once - soon - made - run - gave - open - has - find - only - us - three - our - better - hold - buy - funny - warm - ate - full - those - done - use - fast - say - light - pick - hurt - pull - cut - kind - both - sit - which - fall - carry - small - under - read - why - own - found - wash - slow - hot - because - far - live - draw - clean - grow - best - upon - these - sing - together - please - thank - wish - many - shall - laugh

Learning these words is usually stressed when students are reading at the first- and second-grade levels. And although they were not originally intended for this purpose, Dolch word lists are sometimes used to provide a sense of reading grade level (see chapter 5).

The Fry word list contains a list of the one hundred most frequent words used in children's reading from most frequent to least (the complete list goes all the way up to one thousand most frequent words):

> **Fry Word List.** the - of - and - a - to - in - is - you - that - it - he - was - for - on - are - as - with - his - they - I - at - be - this - have - from -

or - one - had - by - word - but - not - what - all - were - we - when - your - can - said - there - use - an - each - which - she - do - how - their - if - will - up - other - about - out - many - then - them - these - so - some - her - would - make - like - him - into - time - has - look - two - more - write - go - see - number - no - way - could - people - my - than - first - water - been - call - who - oil - its - now - find - long - down - day - did - get - come - made - may - part

The first twenty-five words make up approximately one-third of all the words in printed material (Fry, Kress, & Fountoukidis, 2000). These first one hundred words make up approximately one-half of all the words in printed material that students will encounter.

Using Most Frequent Word Lists

The approach taken to the most frequent word (MFW) lists should be systematic. That is, you should have a general plan to cover all one hundred words (or all 220) and a way to document when students have mastered a word.

The Plan

The simplest way to cover these words is to start at the top and work your way down the list. But how much time and attention should be given to sight words? A couple of thoughts: The first priority in any reading program, whether it be tutoring, remediation, or enrichment programs for gifted learners, should involve reading and enjoy good books. After that, I would estimate that attention to sight words should make up anywhere from five to fifteen minutes of daily reading instruction until the student has mastered the one hundred MFW. Again, this is an estimate. Keep instruction brief, briskly paced, and as enjoyable as possible.

Observe your students to see what sorts of instruction or activities seem to be working. As mentioned earlier in this book, humans are not standardized products. There is no such thing as a magic bullet or secret formula that works best with every student or teacher every time. Instead, there are many tiny magic bullets (some call it magic buckshot) that should be used together. The best strategy in all cases is the one that works.

Documentation

Documentation is merely a matter of keeping track of which words students know. One way to do this is to keep a list for each student you work with and circle the word when it's mastered. Forms like the one below can be created. You can put a check mark to indicate that students are able to recognize the word in print or record the date mastered. Some prefer to record the level of mastery, although this gets more complicated. I recommend keeping things as simple as possible. Keep a list like this one with each student's name on it in a three-ring binder:

Student: _____

____the	____an
____of	____it
____and	____that
____a	____was
____to	____her
____at	____for
____be	____on
____this	____like
____have	____my
____he	____are
____as	____you
____use	____is

Then, simply circle the word as you notice it entering students' reading vocabularies.

Instruction

Initial sight word instruction should involve seeing the word, saying the word, and spelling the word (orally or writing). After this initial instruction, use a variety of games, strategies, and techniques. Some are described in the next section. If you come up with some creative or unique ones, I would be most interested in hearing about them. Send me an e-mail at: andrew.johnson@mnsu.edu. I'll put these in the next edition of this book with your name underneath.

Sight Word Games

This section describes games that can be created using sight words.

Flash cards. Write sight words on 3x5 cards. Use three to seven words in any one setting. These should be words with which you have already done the see-say-spell instruction described above. The key here is to flash the card briefly (hence the name flash cards). Show the word for only one to three seconds. This short exposure helps students to recognize the words quickly when they see it in authentic reading contexts. You can make a variety of flash card games; however, all games should start with the flash exercise. Five of these games are described below:

- *Flash-offs.* When working with two students, have flash-offs to see who can recognize the word first. The student who recognizes the word first gets to keep that card. The winner is the student with the most cards at the end of the round.

- *Flash-Card Rummy.* Use ten to fifteen sight words. Make three cards for each word. Words should be written in three colors. For example, using the word *the*, one should be in red, another black, and another blue. Mix the cards up. Players start with five cards. Just like in the real Rummy, they draw and discard cards. When they get three of a kind, they lay them down and say the sight word. The person who gets rid of all his or her cards first is the winner. You can add more sight word cards as students progress or if you wish to play with three or more players.

- *Concentration.* Have cards in which there are two copies of each sight word used. Again, it is best if they are different colors (a red *the* and a black *the*). Spread them out facedown. Students look for pairs by turning them over. They must say the word as they turn it over. Once they find a pair, they get to keep it. The person with the most pairs at the end of the game is the winner. When you start out use no more than twelve cards.

- *Old Dog.* This is a more politically correct version of Old Maid. The goal is not to be the person left holding the Old Dog card. Create a sight word card deck with three cards for every sight

71

word. Create one card with a funny picture on it (an old dog perhaps). All cards are dealt. Any triads (three of the same cards) in the hand are laid down. Students must say the sight words as they lay the cards down. Then, players take turns drawing from the person on their right. As triads form, they are laid down and the sight words are read out loud. The game ends when all the cards are laid down. The person holding the Old Dog loses.

- *Go Fish.* Just like Flash-Card Rummy and Old Dog, create a deck using ten to fifteen sight words with three cards for each word. The goal is to get rid of all your cards first. If you have a triad, these cards are laid down in front of you. This game works best with three players but can be played with two. Deal six cards to each player putting the rest facedown on the table. Take turns, going clockwise around the table. When it is a player's turn, that player can ask another player for a particular word card. Example: "*Do you have any 'in' cards?*" If that player has any "in" cards he or she must give all of them. If not, the player says, "*Go Fish.*" The original player draws from the deck. The winner is the person who has the most sets of cards at the end of the game.

Crazy Words. This game is similar to Crazy Eights. Create a deck using ten to fifteen sight words with three cards for each word each in a different color. The goal is to get rid of your cards. Deal five cards to each player. Put the rest of the cards facedown, but turn over the top card. Players must lay a card of the same color, or the same word. They must say the word as they lay it down. Pick one word to be a crazy word. (It's fun to let students pick the crazy word.) If you have a crazy word card, it's a wild card in that you can call any color you want. If it's a player's turn and he or she doesn't have the color or a matching word, that person must draw until the correct color is drawn. The first person to get rid of his or her cards is the winner.

Word-O. This game was described in chapter 9. It's played like Bingo using sight words (see figure 10.1).

the	have	it	and
of	in	it	in
an	from	of	the
some	the	and	use

Figure 10.1. Word-O Card for Sight Words

Racing. This game works best with two players but can be played with three. Create a drag strip or a racetrack on a piece of paper or cardboard similar to figure 10.2. The drag strip or track should contain ten to forty spaces. Give students a marker of some kind. (You might create strips and tracks large enough so that Matchbox cars can be used for markers.) Have a deck of sight word cards laying facedown on the table. In turn, players draw a card. They say the word on the card, then move forward the number of letters in the word. After you have played the game

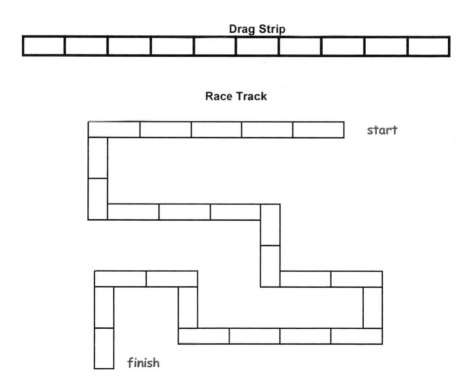

Figure 10.2. Drag Strip and Racetrack for Sight Words

a couple of times let students create their own drag strips and racetracks. As always, encourage creativity. Let them draw in lights, trees, mountains, and other things.

Board games. You can use any board game to reinforce sight words. Instead of dice or a spinner have students draw sight word cards and move their markers forward the number of letters in the word as described above. You could also create sight word cards that have numbers written on them. After drawing a card students must say the word before moving forward that many spaces.

Checkers. Create your own checkerboard using a large sheet of butcher paper. Have students on each side of the checkerboard write sight words on what would be the black squares. Every time a checker is moved to a particular square, the word must be read out loud. Since two players are on opposite sides of the board, each word should be written twice in the square (so the same word is facing each player: one upside down and the other right-side up). In this way the other player can check to see if the word is pronounced correctly.

Word Walls

I briefly described word walls in chapter 8. To remind you, it's simply a list of words that are posted in some form on the wall or bulletin board. Most teachers use butcher paper or poster paper. If you are working with one or two students in a small area, you can use regular printer-size paper. Words walls are used (a) for visual prompts or reference for review, (b) to reinforce letter sounds and sight words, and (c) for quick incidental learning activities.

Categories or groups. Putting all one hundred or 220 sight words on a word wall would be overwhelming. Thus, sight words need to be organized somehow and put up in small groups. Below are some example categories that could be used to display them:

> **Action Words:** put - open - start - buy
> **Other-People Words:** he - she - they - you - them
> **Question Words:** why - how - when - where - who
> **Feeling Words:** hurt - like - thank - happy - sad
> **2-Letter Words:** to - in - he - it - of - in
> **Words with "o" in Them:** to - you - of - for - on - look

Weekly/monthly words. Depending on the level of the student, I would recommend introducing no more than five to ten sight words a week. Display these words by week and month and use them to do written or verbal cloze activities:

September

Week 1	Week 2	Week 3	Week 4
in	was	for	at
is	said	on	him
you	his	they	with
that	that	but	up
it	she	had	all

For example: "I'm thinking of a word in September, week 4 for this sentence. 'I want to go _____ my mom to the store.'" You could also ask students to create oral or written sentences using the words.

Daily sight word. You could also have sight-word-of-the-day displayed on a monthly calendar (figure 10.3). (If you are working with a small group or the whole class this calendar would need to be fairly large.) As a new month starts, tear the old calendar page off and tape it on the wall. This allows you to quickly review the sight words for that month.

Other Strategies or Games

You are limited only by your imagination in how you use these words or work them into games or activities.

September

SUN	MON	TUE	WED	THUR	FRI	SAT
			1 the	2 to	3 and	4 me
5 he	6 a	7 I	8 you	9 it	10 of	11 in
12 was	13 said	14 his	15 that	16 she	17 for	18 on
19 they	20 but	21 had	22 at	23 him	24 with	25 up
26 all	27 look	28 is	29 her	30 there	31 some	

Figure 10.3. Sight Word Calendar

Writing prompts.   Use writing prompts with one or more sight words. For example, to reinforce "outside" and "saw," your writing prompt would be: "Outside I saw _____." Children would finish the sentence and then tell you (or write) what they saw outside.

Picture sentences.   To complete a writing prompt, younger students may use a picture sentence or picture story. This is where students draw a picture to complete the sentence. A teacher, parent, tutor, or paraprofessional then asks each student to tell his or her picture sentence. The students' sentences are then written on their pictures. Figure 10.4 shows a picture sentence (a picture story would be two to five sentences). Collect a number of these and make them into a book to use in practicing reading. The picture cues and personal connections enable students to successfully read things that they have written and, at the same time, practice and reinforce sight words.

Word sorts.   Give children six to ten words at a time (more for older children) written on 3x5 inch cards. They are then asked to sort the words into groups. Each word can belong in only one group. Some examples of word sorts with sight words are show below:

Words with "i" in them: I, it, in, said, his
Words with "s" in them: said, his, she
1-letter words: I, a
2-letter words: he, to
3-letter words: the, and, you

Figure 10.4.   Picture Sentence

Outside I saw a bike.

Action words: get, look, make, off, play
Place words: in, up

Treasure hunts.   The treasure hunts described in chapter 9 can also be used with sight words.

IN   OF   THE   WHERE

Like before, students can create tables or graphs with the data they find. They can also compare one story to another.

Words with distracters.   This is an activity or game to practice seeing sight words. Give students a sheet of paper with three words placed in a box or list:

in - the - most
ran - of - up
my - can - go
what - where - big

Two of the words are distracters. Say one of the words. The student must point to the word and say it. If you want to make a game out of it, make a set of twenty boxes or words and time students to see how fast they can find the words. Do this three times in a row. Record their time each round. This will enable them to see their time decrease.

Sight word pictures.   Sight word pictures are used as visual references to remember a particular sight word. Here students create a short phrase or partial sentence using a sight word and draw a picture to remind them of the word (see figure 10.5). These can be posted in the room or used to create a sight word book.

Choral reading.   Create a simple sentence or two written on a large sheet of paper (or single piece of paper if you are working with one or two students). Make sure the sentences are about the students or connected to their lives or experiences. Read each sentence together out loud. Point to each word as it is read. Ask students if they notice any sight words after each sentence or go back and point out the sight words to reinforce them.

Echo reading.   Similar to choral reading, create a sentence or two that is displayed so all students can see it. Read each sentence out loud to students, pointing to each word as you read. Then have students read or echo the sentence back to you as you point to each word.

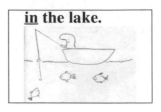

Figure 10.5. Sight Word with Picture

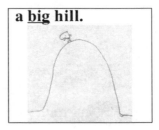

Wide reading.   Wide reading is the cure for almost everything related to literacy. Make sure you have many good books around the room with lots of pictures in short, single sentences. Cartoons or comic strips can also be effective to use here.

Internet Search Terms

Sight words: *sight-words, sight-word-activities, sight-word-games, most-frequent-word-list, most-frequent-words, Fry-list, Dolch-words, Dolch-list, instant-words.*

References

Fry, E. B., Kress, J. E., & Fountoukidis, D. L. (2000) *The reading teacher's book of lists* (third ed.). San Francisco: Jossey-Bass.

DEVELOPING FLUENCY

R eading fluency is the ability to recognize words automatically. Automatic word recognition improves comprehension by allowing the reader to use more thinking space focusing on the meaning of the message instead of letters and individual words (Kuder & Hasit, 2002). Reading fluency also means reading quickly. Why is rate important? A homework assignment that would take average readers about twenty minutes to read and comprehend might take a struggling reader forty to sixty minutes (Allington, 2006). This means that low ability readers might have to spend twice as long completing homework and other assignments. This makes it far less likely that they will be completed or completed very well.

This chapter describes strategies that can be used to enhance reading fluency. Many are based on strategies found in Richard Allington's (2006) book, *What Really Matters for Struggling Readers: Designing Research-Based Programs*. I would heartily recommend this book along with the others listed below:

Allington, R. L. (2006). *What really matters for struggling readers: Designing research-based programs* (second ed.). Boston: Allyn and Bacon.

Atwell, N. (1998). *In the middle: New understanding about writing, reading, and learning* (second ed.). Portsmouth, N.H.: Heinemann.

Cunningham, P. M. (2005). *Phonics they use: words for reading and writing* (fourth ed.). Boston: Allyn and Bacon.

Cunningham, P. M., & Allington, R. L. (2007). *Classrooms that work: They can all read and write.* Boston: Allyn and Bacon.

Goodman, K. (1986). *What's whole in whole language?* Richmond Hill, Ontario, Canada: Scholastic.

Graves, D. (1983). *Writing: Teachers and children at work.* Portsmouth, N.H.: Heinemann.

Hansen, J. (2001). *When writers read* (second ed.). Portsmouth, N.H.: Heinemann.

Kuder, S. J., & Hasit, C. (2002). *Enhancing literacy for all students.* Upper Saddle River, N.J.: Merrill, Prentice Hall.

Routman, R. (2003). *Reading essentials: The specifics you need to teach reading well.* Portsmouth, N.H.: Heinemann.

Routman, R. (2005). *Writing essentials: Raising expectations and results while simplifying teaching.* Portsmouth, N.H.: Heinemann.

Weaver, C. (2002). *Reading process and practice* (third ed.). Portsmouth, N.H.: Heinemann.

Zemelman, S., Daniels, H., & Hyde, A. (2006). *Best practice: New standards for teaching and learning in America's schools* (third ed.). Portsmouth, N.H.: Heinemann.

One-on-One Tutorial Activities to Develop Fluency

The fluency activities described in this section are designed for individual tutoring or teaching sessions. However, after some practice students could work with a buddy, thereby enabling you to do these activities with small groups of students. They should be done no more than once a day in sessions lasting no more than five to ten minutes.

Repeated Reading

Why do musicians spend hours practicing scales? It's to develop fluency. Their goal is to be able to see notes of music on the page and automatically process and play them. Repeated reading is a strategy based on this same concept whereby students improve their ability to recognize and process letter patterns through reoccurring practice (Samuels, 2002). It can be done with a tutor in a one-on-one or small group setting, or with a buddy in a whole class group setting.

Start by finding a piece of text that is within students' independent reading levels. The text should be a minimum of 120 to 150 words. On a starting command, students start reading as fast as they can for one minute (you may want to use thirty to forty-five seconds for primary age students). The goal is for them to pronounce as many words as they can in that time period. We're not concerned with comprehension here, simply pronouncing each word. Then, follow along as the student reads to make sure every word is pronounced. Give hints or cues when necessary. Use a stopwatch to keep time. Call "stop" at the end of the allotted time. The number of words the student read per minute is then counted and recorded. (Hint: Use reading samples with every ten words marked off for easy counting.) This process is repeated twice more. Finally, students record their three WPM scores (words per minute) on a line graph (see figure 11.1).

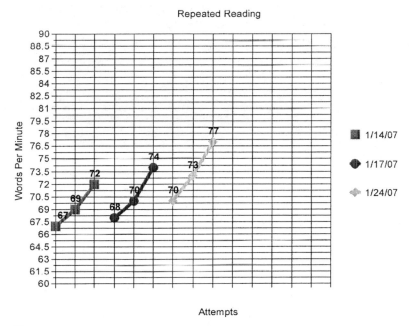

Figure 11.1. Repeated Reading Graph

Some like to record the number of errors per minute (EPM) as well as the words per minute (WPM); however, I find this not in keeping with the overall aim of repeated reading, which is to develop reading fluency and to find a positive way for students to demonstrate growth and progress in reading. Indeed, one of the strengths of this research-based strategy is that students are able to experience success. They're able to see progress as their scores go up from their first to their third attempt. This serves to improve their sense of self-efficacy (believing they can accomplish things with effort), which in turn has a positive effect on academic achievement (Eggen & Kauchak, 2007).

This question is often asked of me: Do you use the same piece of graded reading every session? Or do you change? Let me answer this way: Some students desperately need to experience success. They come to school and because of learning difficulties, find themselves failing for six hours straight. Could you imagine how you'd feel if you were forced to experience failure day after day? Is it any wonder that students with learning difficulties often seem not to be motivated? ("Oh goodie, I get to go to school and fail for six hours again. I can't wait.") And doesn't it make sense that disruptive behavior (acting out) is perhaps the healthiest response to an unhealthy situation? If you have a student who needs to experience success, meet that need. Use the same piece of writing over several consecutive sessions. Below are the steps for repeated reading:

1. Find a piece of text at students' independent level.

2. Students read as fast as they can for one minute.

3. Teacher checks to make sure no words were skipped. Gives hints when necessary.

4. Stop and record number of words read (have prenumbered pieces of text).

5. Repeat the process two more times. Record the number of words read in one minute.

6. Students record their scores on a line graph in a portfolio.

Reread to Meet Goal

This strategy invites students to work to meet a goal (thereby helping to develop both fluency and a sense of self-efficacy). Start by finding students' approximate WPM scores when reading at their independent reading level. Then set goals for students that are slightly above this level. For example, if a student's average WPM is 75, set a goal for the student to read 78 WPM. Then, using a piece of text that is at that student's independent reading level, see how many attempts it takes the student to read the text in order to reach the WPM goal. Record the number of attempts:

Date: 1/12/08
Goal: 75 WPM
Number of tries: 5

Date: 1/21/08
Goal: 78 WPM
Number of tries: 6

Date: 1/14/08
Goal: 75 WPM
Number of tries: 3

Date: 1/26/08
Goal: 78 WPM
Number of tries: 5

Date: 1/18/08
Goal: 75 WPM
Number of tries: 2

Date: 1/29/08
Goal: 78 WPM
Number of tries: 3

I have found that graphs, being more visually oriented, are generally more motivating for students to use to record their progress in these types of activities (figure 11.2).

Below are the specific steps for rereading to meet a goal:

1. Determined approximate WPM on graded writing.

2. Set a goal slightly above approximate WPM.

3. Students read selected (at independent reading level) text for one minute.

4. Stop and record number of words read (use prenumbered pieces of text).

5. Repeat the process until student has met WPM goal.

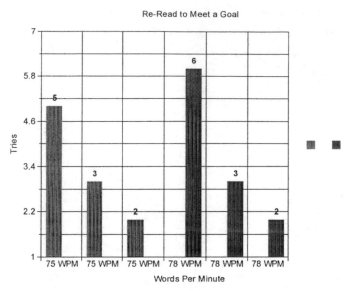

Figure 11.2.   **Bar Graph for Reread to Meet a Goal**

6. Students record their number of attempts using a table or bar graph in a portfolio.

Timed Reading

Timed reading is similar to repeated reading. First give students a one-hundred-word passage. (It works best to count off one hundred words in a familiar book or a longer piece of reading.) The selection used here should again be at students' independent reading levels. Then have students read the one-hundred-word passage as fast as they can three times successively. Record the time it takes them to read it after each attempt. (Students should see their times going down slightly after each reading.) Finally, have students record their three reading times in a portfolio:

Date: 1/12/08
1. 75 seconds
2. 70 seconds
3. 69 seconds

Date: 1/14/08
1. 75 seconds
2. 69 seconds
3. 68 seconds

Date: 1/18/08
1. 74 seconds
2. 69 seconds
3. 62 seconds

For a more visual display, use a bar graph (figure 11.3) or line graph (figure 11.1). To enable students to experience success, I would again recommend using the same piece of reading material over several successive sessions.

Below are the specific steps for timed reading:

1. Find a piece of reading at a student's independent level.

2. Count off a one-hundred-word section.

3. Student reads the selection three times.

4. Record the time for each attempt.

5. Final results are documented on a table, graph, or chart.

Replay Analysis

First, find a sample of graded reading of about 100 or 120 words. This should be at students' instructional levels. Photocopy the reading so that

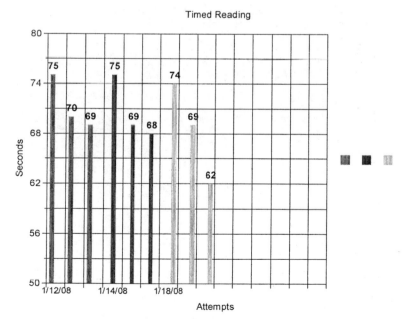

Figure 11.3. Bar Graph Used for Timed Reading

students can make marks on it. Next, students read the selection out loud into a tape recorder. After reading, students replay and analyze their oral reading along with the teacher to look for errors or mispronunciations. (Listening to the tape helps students determine what makes sense in the context of each sentence. Since they do not have to focus on decoding words, they are able to concentrate on meaning. They are thus able to use both context and meaning to detect errors or mispronunciations.) In this first analysis, mispronounced words are noted by putting a small X over them. The oral reading, taping, and analysis are repeated two more times. During the second analysis, mispronounced words are noted with a √ mark. During the third analysis, they are noted with a + sign. Students are able to see the number of errors go down after each reading. They can then document the numbers of errors using a table or graph.

Below are the specific steps for replay analysis:

1. Photocopy a reading selection (instructional level).

2. Students read selection out loud. Audiotape their reading.

3. Replay tape, check for errors (analysis).

4. First time, denote errors with an X.

5. Repeat oral reading, taping, and analysis.

6. Second time, denote errors with a ✓.

7. Repeat oral reading, taping, and analysis.

8. Third time, denote errors with a +.

9. Use a table or graph to document the total number of errors. (Example: 7 - 3 - 1)

Small Group and Whole Class Activities to Develop Fluency

Described in this section are four activities that can be used to develop fluency when working with small groups of students or the whole class.

Choral Reading

Choral reading is reading a piece of text together (in a chorus). The advantage of reading this way is that students have instant sound cues for words they may not recognize immediately. Choral reading is done most often in primary grades where the teacher reads from a big book. A big book is a book that's big—at least three feet high. There are usually one or two sentences per page, written in large letters so that a group of children, sitting on the floor around the teacher, is able to see them. The teacher has a pointer and points to each word as the class reads together. Choral reading can also be used with the language experience approach described in chapter 6.

The goal. The goal of choral reading, like all strategies described in this chapter, is to strengthen neuron pathways to make letter sound and word identification microseconds quicker. It should be one of many strategies used; however, it should not become your sole means of reading instruction. Neither should this strategy be used for reading assigned textbook chapters. For example, it would be an inappropriate use of choral reading to have students read an entire chapter in their social studies book. This is a fluency strategy, not a comprehension strategy.

With older students, choral reading can be done with individuals or groups using regular sized books. Here each student has a book or a photocopied piece of the text. Students should then move their finger along with the text as they read to keep them focused.

Creative options. There are a variety of creative options using poetry to create a type of spoken choral work. Song lyrics, something that might appeal to older students, can also be used as a source for choral reading. The purpose here is to create a performance piece. Three possible performing venues:

- Students love to perform in front of other students. This can be done as part of all-school programs. You can also visit individual classrooms. This allows students to perform their choral works more than one time.

- Students love to perform for parents. This could be at an open house, or as part of a school music or art program.

- Create audiotapes that can be played with books. This makes stories come alive for young students.

- Create videotapes for in-school cable or community cable broadcast.

The Internet search terms at the end of the chapter can be used to get more ideas for performance and other creative options related to choral reading.

The process.   Start by selecting a poem. While narrative text can be used as well, poems are usually easier. Use something that's short and simple that students will enjoy, such as Mother Goose, Shel Silverstein, and Dr. Seuss books. Then start arranging lines, breaking them into parts, solos, duets, and small groups.

Alternating voices.   When designing a poem for choral reading, have students use a variety of voices when reading different lines or sections. This is what makes choral reading fun. Below are some ideas for alternating or arranging voices within the choral reading performance:

1. Use high voice or low voice.

2. Pause.

3. Speed up or slow down.

4. Include noises, claps, stomps, or funny sounds.

5. Repeat lines.

6. Assign character voices.

7. Alternate feeling: sad voice, happy voice, angry voice, funny voice, questioning voice.

8. Vary volume: loud voice, soft voice.

9. Alternate lines: smooth flowing line, or bumpy, attacking, staccato.

10. Assign individual or groups of students to specific lines or voices.

11. Assign solo and duet lines.

12. Add interesting comments or lines.

13. Include movement: hands, head, feet, bodies.

An example. I've included an example of a simple nursery rhyme that I've arranged for a choral reading performance. I would encourage you start with some simple nursery rhymes like this. Print the words on a chart or create individual scripts. Then model how the voices should sound in each line and then assign parts.

Hickory Dickory Dock
All: Hickory Dickory Dock,
Billy and Sally: Tick, tock, tick, tock, tick, tock.
All: The mouse . . .
Girls: Squeak, squeak. (quietly, with a high voice)
All: ran up . . .
Boys: (make huffing and puffing sounds)
All: the clock.
Stewart: Gong! (loud, shouting voice)
Billy and Sally: Tick, tock, tick, tock, tick tock. (flat, boring, monotone voice)
All: The clock struck one,
Patty: Ow! That hurts. (whining sound)
All: The mouse . . .
Girls: Squeak, squeak. (quietly, with a high voice)
All: ran down . . .
Boys: Down, down, down, down. (voices getting lower)
Girls: How low can you go, how low can you go, how low can you go . . . (voices getting quieter)
All: Hickory Dickory Dock.
Billy and Sally: Tick, tock, tick, tock, tick tock.
Pause . . .
All: What's a Dickory? (loud questioning)

Keep initial choral readings performances simple and short. After you have done several of these, you might include students in the arranging process. Get their ideas for breaking it up and adding interesting voices and lines. After students get comfortable with this form, a natural extension would be use of creative movement, gestures, and eventually dance. And of course, students will eventually want to create and design their own choral reading performances.

Echo Reading

Echo reading is where the teacher reads a line of text and students repeat or echo it. This can be done with a big book or regular-size books (described previously). As students echo back the line, the teacher should point to the words as they read them. To enhance fluency, echo read the same piece two or three times, moving faster each time. Echo reading can also be used with the language experience approach described in chapter 6.

Reader's Theater—Radio Drama

In reader's theater, students take a familiar story (one they have read) and break it into parts, creating a script. I sometimes call these radio dramas as it helps students envision an audience. Stories are then broken into scripts with students assigned to different parts. Use narrator and character parts. You can also use students for sound effects. Students will eventually be able to create their own radio dramas from familiar stories. These can be audiotaped for use with picture books. Here's an example of how a story might be arranged into a reader's theater script:

Narrator: Once upon a time, three pigs lived with their mother. One morning Mother Pig said to the three pigs.

Mother Pig: Pigs! Your rooms are dirty and messy. You never clean up after yourself. You live like a bunch of pigs.

Narrator: The smartest of the three pigs, Patty, said.

Patty Pig: But we are pigs, mother.

Mother Pig: That's it. Out with you. Go out and build your own house.

Narrator: So the three pigs, Patty, Peter, and Peggy, went out into the world to build a house.

Repeated Reading for Small or Large Groups

Repeated reading can also be done as a whole class or small group activity. Here students are grouped in pairs. As the first student reads, the second checks to make sure no words are skipped. Also, in small and large groups I have found that it works best for students to read a selection twice instead of three times. With large group repeated reading you will want to have three or four different text selections for students to read. In this way, the readers won't get confused if they hear a neighbor reading just ahead of or behind them out loud. Below are the specific steps to use when doing repeated reading with a whole class or small groups of students:

1. Find a piece of text at grade level.

2. Put students into pairs.

3. Student #1 reads as fast as he or she can for one minute. Student #2 checks to make sure that no words were skipped.

4. Stop and record number of words read (have prenumbered pieces of text).

5. Repeat the process with student #1 again reading. Record the number of words read in one minute.

6. Put scores on a graph in a portfolio and switch roles (student #2 reads).

Internet Search Terms

Fluency: *reading-fluency, fluency-instruction, developing-reading-fluency, reading-fluency-activities, assessing-reading-fluency.*

Repeated reading: *repeated-reading, repeated-reading-strategies, repeated-reading-activities.*

Reader's theater: *readers-theater-activities, readers-theater.*

Choral reading: *choral-reading, choral-reading-strategies, unison-reading, unison-reading-strategies, poems-choral-reading.*

References

Allington, R. L. (2006) *What really matters for struggling readers: Designing research-based programs* (second ed.). Boston: Allyn and Bacon.

Eggen, P., & Kauchak, D. (2007) *Educational psychology: Windows on classrooms* (seventh ed.). Upper Saddle River, N.J.: Pearson.

Kuder, S. J., & Hasit, C. (2002) *Enhancing literacy for all students.* Upper Saddle River, N.J.: Merrill, Prentice Hall.

Samuels, S. J. (2002) Reading fluency: Its development and assessment. In A. Farstrup and S. J. Samuels (Eds.), *What research has to say about reading instruction* (166–83). Newark, Del.: International Reading Association.

CHAPTER TWELVE
VOCABULARY

Vocabulary instruction is used to help students learn new words and to help them acquire a deeper understanding of the words they know. Attending to students' vocabularies is an important part of enhancing their ability to read, write, speak, listen, and think. Why? Word knowledge affects students' ability to comprehend what they read, which in turn helps them expand their knowledge base, which in turn facilitates their vocabulary growth, which in turn enhances their ability to comprehend what they read, which in turn . . . (you get the picture).

Four Vocabularies

We have four different vocabularies:

Listening vocabulary are the words we hear and understand, commonly referred to as words we know. This is the largest of our vocabularies and the one upon which the others are built.

Speaking vocabulary are the words we use in conversation. Our listening vocabulary is larger than our speaking vocabulary because our understanding of some words is incomplete or contextual (we understand a word in the context of a sentence or situation, but not necessarily by itself). Thus, adding both depth and dimension to our word knowledge enables us to express our thoughts more efficiently and effectively.

Reading vocabulary are the words that we are able to read. Most students enter school with very few words in their reading vocabulary. To this, they add approximately three thousand new words a year (Anderson & Nagy, 1992). As stated earlier in this book, learning to read is much easier if students are reading words in their listening and speaking vocabularies. Thus, increasing the number of words in students' listening vocabularies makes learning to read easier.

Writing vocabulary are the words we use to express ourselves in written form. This is usually the smallest of the four vocabularies. We write using only those words we can read and understand. Just like listening and speaking vocabularies, our reading vocabulary is larger than our writing vocabulary.

Conversation and Teaching

We can help expand students' knowledge base as well as their listening vocabularies simply by conversing with students (talking with, not to). Yes, conversation can be considered a research-based strategy (Baumann, Kameʻenui, & Ash, 2003). However, the new words you use in these conversations should be attached to known words and concepts.

NEW WORDS

known words
known concepts

In the same way, when teaching new concepts always connect them to known words and concepts.

NEW CONCEPTS

known words
known concepts

Effective Vocabulary Instruction

Students learn approximately three thousand words each year. By the end of elementary school they know approximately twenty-five thousand and by the end of high school approximately fifty thousand words (Harp & Brewer, 2005). But how do students learn all these words? Is it possible to teach fifty thousand words through direct instruction and vocabulary worksheets? If not, what strategies are effective in enhancing word knowledge?

Ineffective Approaches to Vocabulary Instruction

Let's first start by describing what *not* to do. Susanne Barchers (1998) describes common strategies that are not very effective:

Writing dictionary definitions.   Looking up words in a dictionary (or glossary) and having students write the definition is ineffective and a poor use of precious educational minutes. This is because the words are usually presented outside a meaningful context. As well, dictionary definitions tend to use words and descriptions that are rarely connected to students' lives or experiences.

Using vocabulary worksheets with teacher definitions.   Providing teacher definitions of new words and then asking students to complete vocabulary worksheets is also not very effective in enhancing students' depth and breadth of word knowledge.

Memorizing word lists.   Memorizing lists of words and their definitions does very little to enhances students' knowledge of words. Again, words are usually presented outside a meaningful context and simply hearing a definition doesn't result in a deep understanding of the word.

Sentence writing.   Asking students to write sentences using a new word as an isolated exercise is not very effective. The sentences are usually contrived and reflect the singular definition given.

If these strategies are so ineffective, why are they used so often in schools? Perhaps it's because they haven't read my book?

Features of Effective Vocabulary Instruction

Susan Watts (1995) describes six features of effective vocabulary instruction. Each is listed here with some simple strategies for its application. And remember, strategies do not need to be complicated or cumbersome to be rigorous and effective.

Multiple exposures.   In your teaching and tutoring sessions, you can call attention to new or interesting words, but this initial exposure does very little to move the new word into students' listening or speaking vocabularies. Instead, students must encounter new words in a variety of contexts over time.

Meaningful context. Words used for vocabulary instruction should be connected to students' lives or experiences to the greatest extent possible. Also, look to present new words in the context of a common story, theme, or curriculum content area being studied.

Prior knowledge. New words should always be introduced in the context of known words and concepts. Before introducing a new word, first ask students to identify things they know about the related topic. For example, when introducing the word *magnetism*, a teacher would ask, "What are some things you know about magnets?" Students' ideas would be listed on the board. The teacher would then say, "Our new word today is magnetism. See if you can guess what it might mean from this sentence: 'Magnetism caused the steel rod to move toward the magnet.'" The teacher would then ask, "From this sentence, what do you think magnetism might mean?" The teacher would get students' answers before using kid language to define it: "Magnetism is what we call the invisible force that pulls iron or steel things to a magnet."

Relationships or connections. Show the relationship or make the connection between new words and known words or concepts. For example, to introduce the word *transportation* a teacher would say, "Transportation comes from transport. To transport means moving a person or thing from one place to another. For example, I can transport myself from my home to school using my car. I can transport groceries from the store to my house. To transport is to move something. Transportation is the form of moving things. Who can tell me other forms of transportation?" Semantic maps can also be used to visually show relationships (figure 12.1.).

An SA (synonym and association) chart can also be used to show relationships. For example, *inquisitive* means curious, snooping, asking questions, wants to know, nosy. In the first column, synonyms are listed. In the second column students list things they associate with the new word (it words best for students to work in pairs or small groups here).

Mary is very <u>inquisitive.</u>	**ASSOCIATIONS**
SYNONYMS	- Wrapped birthday presents
curious	- A good mystery. What happens next?
snooping	- A detective
asking questions	- None of his business
wants to know	- Gossip
nosy	- A really interesting class

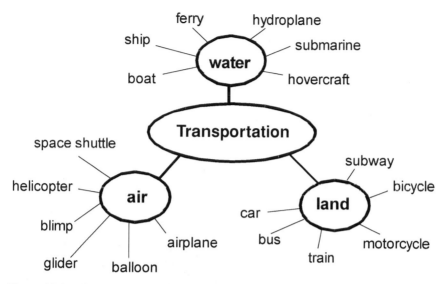

Figure 12.1. Semantic Map to Show Relationships

Context clues and dictionaries. The use of context clues was described fairly extensively in chapter 7. By itself, it's of little value. Instead, it should be combined with teaching students how to look up words in the dictionary. In this computer age, there are two other strategies that you should be teaching students. First, do an Internet search using the target word followed by "define" or "definition." This is the quickest way to get many definitions. Second, use the synonym feature in the Tools function of your word processing program. For example, not knowing exactly what "onus" might mean, teach students to type it into a document and click the synonym function. If you did this you'd get the following words: responsibility, obligation, burden, and duty. This provides a good sense of what the word might mean.

Seeing, saying, and using them. When encountering new words, make sure students see them (in the context of a sentence), say them, and then use them in a written or oral context. But simply asking students to write or say a sentence using the new word can often result in an abstract, meaningless pile of mush. However, there is a better way. It's what I call the *parallel prompt.* This is a writing prompt that gets students using the new word in the context of their own lives or experiences. For example, if I were introducing the word *onus,* a parallel prompt would ask students to describe something for which they are responsible in their lives. They would be asked to finish the sentence, "In my life, the onus is on me to . . ."

Strategies for Developing Students' Vocabularies

Based on the features of effective vocabulary instruction described above, six strategies or activities for developing students' vocabularies are presented here:

Word walls.   Use word walls to display words in context (see chapter 8). For example, display new science words in the context of a particular concept (rain, weather, sleet, evaporation, water cycle, etc.) or arrange them in categories around a particular theme or story. This provides a context for seeing new words and presents a visual reference for reviewing ideas covered in previous lessons. As well, use words from the word wall for quick games, riddles, or sponge activities.

Semantic maps.   Semantic maps or word webs display new words in a way that shows their relationship to other words or ideas (figure 12.2). In the same way, words can be displayed in context using pictures, diagrams, labels, or charts.

Wide reading.   Reading is the best practice for learning to read (Allington, 2000). Wide reading is also the most productive method for building vocabulary (Nagy & Herman, 1987). Wide reading exposes students to more words, increases word recognition and reading fluency, facilitates word learning, and helps to expand students' knowledge base.

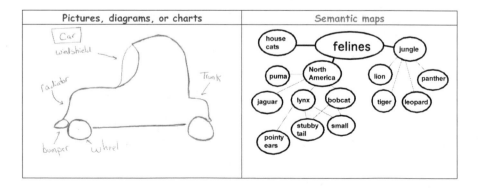

Figure 12.2.   Pictures, Diagrams, Charts, and Semantic Maps

Thus, an effective homework assignment for a literacy class would be to ask students to simply find a good book and enjoy it for ten to fifteen minutes every night. For grading purposes, give points for completion and maintenance of the reading log.

Reading Homework Assignment Log
Enjoyment Level Key: 10 = very high enjoyment; 5 = average enjoyment;
   1 = very low enjoyment

Book: *Brian's Winter*
Date: Jan. 12, 2008
Time: 7:00–7:20 p.m.
Pages: 118–122
Enjoyment level: 8

Book: *Brian's Winter*
Date: Jan. 13, 2008
Time: 7:05–7:25 p.m
Pages: 122–130
Enjoyment level: 10

Book: *Where the Red Fern Grows*
Date: Jan. 14, 2008
Time: 7:00–7:30 p.m.
Pages: 1–20
Enjoyment level: 8

Journals. Journals (often called literature logs, reading logs, or reading journals) can be used for pre- and postreading activities (instead of expensive consumable workbooks). These are simply empty notebooks that students use to record a variety of things (see chapters 14, 15, and 16), including the reading homework assignment log just illustrated.

In using a journal for vocabulary development, first identify (or ask students to identify) interesting or important words found in the context of a story or text (usually two to five words depending on the level of the student). Then, have students record the sentence in which they were found in their journal. Finally, have them generate one or two other possible words or phrases that might be substituted for the original word. (If you are tutoring one student, this is something you would do together.)

Have dictionaries, thesauruses, or computers available for students to use in finding synonyms.

Teacher language.   Model the use of new words and precise language when speaking with students in the classroom or tutoring environment. Be conscious of bringing new words into the classroom vocabulary and using them across the curriculum. Over time, use these new words in as many settings and situations as you can.

Word interest.   Create an interest in words. Recognize interesting word usage encountered in text or that you hear in the media. Ask students to be on the lookout for new or interesting words. Have a place on a bulletin board or word wall for new and interesting words. Help students begin to notice how words are arranged to create varied effects. Also, point out interesting or effective ways that writers use words to create feelings, communicate an idea, or describe an event.

Other Strategies

The strategies described here are based on ideas from Suzanne Barchers's (1998) book, *Reading: From Process to Practice*. I recommend this text as a valuable source for help in understanding literacy and literacy instruction.

Connect two.   This is a prereading/postreading activity. It can also be used as a form of an advanced organizer for an expository lesson in science, social studies, or other curriculum area. This small group activity is designed to build upon students' current knowledge. Here are the steps:

1. Identify a list of target vocabulary words related to the story or lesson. List them in column A.

2. Identify a related word for each of the target words. List them in a parallel column.

3. In small groups, students connect the words and state the reason for their connections.

4. As a postreading or postlesson activity, students make necessary corrections.

5. Extend by asking students to create a third column (connect three).

Connect Two

Column A	**Column B**
VOCABULARY	studying
SEMANTIC	wide reading
VARIATION	recognizable
MORPHEMIC	young children
AUTOMATICITY	teacher choice
ONUS	context clues
ECHO READING	fluency
PHONOGRAMS	prefix
SIGHT WORDS	most frequent

Word sort. This activity is also used to add depth and dimension to existing word knowledge and build upon students' current knowledge base. It can be used as a prereading or postreading activity, although it is most effective when used as a postreading or postlesson activity. Here are the steps:

1. Develop a list of important target words. If using as part of pre-/postreading activity, use vocabulary words.

2. Write words on 3x5 cards and show them to students before reading the story.

3. After reading the story, students work in small groups to put the words in logical categories.

4. Students label or identify the categories.

5. Students identify their categories and the number of words found in each.

Vocabulary rating. This is a pre-/postreading activity for small groups. The important part of this is the discussion that arises from student interaction. Here are the steps:

1. As a prereading or prelesson activity, present a list of target words in the rating matrix or in list form.

2. Students meet in small groups to determine the extent of their groups' word knowledge.

3. Students read the chapter (or partake in the lesson).

4. As a postreading or postlesson activity, students meet in small groups and once again rate their groups' word knowledge using a different colored pencil or marker.

Vocabulary Rating
Key: 4 = *can define*, 3 = *have heard*, 2 = *not sure*, 1 = *new word*
____ Onus
____ Invariably
____ Automaticity
____ Logographic

PRE   POST
____ Onus ____
____ Invariably ____
____ Automaticity ____
____ Logographic ____

The Silent Spot and the Noisy Spot.   These are both variations on charades. Both of these games work best with teams of two to five students. It should be used as a postreading activity to reinforce vocabulary. These are the steps for the Silent Spot game:

1. Prepare a list of targeted vocabulary words.

2. Students are put into teams of three to five (four is best).

3. By turn, one member from each team is selected to be a word master. The word master's job is to get his or her team to say the vocabulary word. Clues can consist of noises, nonverbal clues, and physical actions—but no words.

4. The team has fifteen seconds to guess the word (shorter duration for older students, longer duration for younger students). Team members shout out words until the correct word is spoken. If they say the word, they receive one point. If they miss the word, the group whose turn is next confers. They have one guess. If guessed correctly, they steal the point. (If they miss,

the next group in line gets a chance to steal until you are back to the original group.)

5. Continue on with the next team. The first team to earn ten points (or some designated number) is the winner.

6. The last round should be a bonus round where each word is worth two points. This gives teams who are behind the opportunity to catch up. For example, if they got their own two-point bonus question and stole the bonus questions of two other groups, they would have six extra points in this round.

These are the steps for the Noisy Spot game:

1. Noisy Spot is played the same way as Silent Spot, except this time the word master can give word clues. The word master can use sentences along with words and physical gestures—but may not use the word or any form of the word. If the word master accidentally slips and uses the word, the next team in line gets one point.

2. Just like above, if a team does not guess the word in fifteen seconds (shorter duration for older students, longer duration for younger students), the team next in line has a chance to steal the point.

Two Strategies for Moving Words into Productive Vocabulary

The strategies described here are used to help clarify and enrich the meanings of known words, moving words into students' productive vocabularies (they actually use them).

Classifying

Classifying can be used to support students' use and exploration of word dimension. Classifying is used to arrange items or information into a given set of categories. It is a variation of word sort described above. These are the steps:

1. Identify two words that may be new to the students. Ideally, these words are related to or found in a story being read or a unit or lesson being studied in another class. This provides a context for learning the new words.

2. Prepare three to ten synonyms or associations for each of the new words and print them on 3x5 cards. The synonyms can be words, phrases, or associations and should be fairly familiar to students.

3. Introduce each new word (either orally or in writing), in the context of a sentence. Using the context provided, students make guesses as to the word's meaning.

4. Following this, provide an explicit definition of the word and another example of that word being used.

5. When all the new words have been introduced in this fashion, put the two new words on a table or on the front chalkboard as category headings. Students are then informed they have some familiar words that are related to the new words on the board. Give various students one 3x5 card with the synonym or association printed on it. They must then decide which category to put their 3x5 card in and tell why. As this is done, they bring their card up and put it underneath or next to one of the new category words. (This step can be done in large group or small group.)

6. When all the words are posted in their correct categories, students have a visual reference showing the new words and various synonyms and association.

Super Word Web

The Super Word Web (SWW) is variation of the SA chart described above. Its purpose is to develop depth and dimension of word knowledge. This can be used to introduce new vocabulary words as either a prereading or postreading activity. For expository text, it is recommended as a pre-reading activity so that new words and concepts can be used to facilitate comprehension. For narrative text, it is recommended as a postreading activity so that students can use the context of the story to enrich their word knowledge. SWW can be conducted in large or small group, although it should be modeled a number of times before students attempt to use it in small groups.

Here, you again introduce the word, either orally or in writing, in the context of a sentence (see figure 12.3). The teacher provides a definition or, when working in small groups, students use a dictionary. Synonymous words and phrases are listed inside the box. Associations are then listed along the outside of the box. Students can create their SWW on butcher paper for display in the classroom or in their reading logs or learning journals. Encourage students to be creative in the shape of the word box when listing synonyms. For example, if the word was a Halloween word, the

Steps
1. See the word in context.
2. List three or four synonyms or defining phrases inside the figure.
3. List or draw three or four associations.
4. Use in pairs or small groups – create poster or journal entry.

EXAMPLE: *effortlessly*

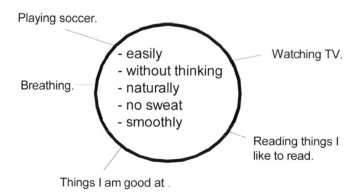

Figure 12.3. Super Word Web

synonyms could be put inside a shape of a pumpkin or ghost. Also, encourage students to draw pictures of their associations. In this way, you bring multiple modes of thinking to the study of words as well as visual references.

Final Thoughts

Word knowledge affects students' ability to learn and comprehend what they read. The goals of effective vocabulary instruction then are to expand students' vocabularies, strengthen their depth and dimension of word knowledge, and move new words into their productive vocabularies. All the strategies described here can be used to this end.

Internet Search Terms

Vocabulary: *vocabulary-instruction, vocabulary-instruction-teachers, vocabulary-activities, vocabulary-lessons, vocabulary-learning.*

Semantic maps: *semantic-maps, semantic-mapping, semantic-maps-teacher, semantic-maps-relationships, semantic-mapping-vocabulary, semantic-maps-concepts, semantic-maps-reading, semantic-maps-reading-instruction.*

Word sorts: *word-sorts, word-sorting, word-sorts-vocabulary, word-sorts-reading-instruction, word-study, word-sorts-teacher, word-sort-activities.*

Other: *word-game-activities, word-games-reading-instruction, vocabulary-games-teachers.*

References

Allington, R. (2000) *What really matters for struggling readers.* New York: Allyn and Bacon.

Anderson, R. C., & Nagy, W. E. (1992) The vocabulary conundrum. *American Educator, 16,* 44–47.

Barchers, S. (1998) *Reading: From process to practice.* Belmont, Calif.: Wadsworth Publishing.

Baumann, J. F., Kame'enui, E. J., & Ash, G. E. (2003) Research on vocabulary instruction: Voltaire redux. In J. Flood, D. Lapp, J. R. Squire, & J. M. Jensen (Eds.),

Handbook on research on teaching the English language arts (second ed., 752–85). Mahwah, N.J.: Erlbaum.

Graves, M. (1986) Costs and benefits of different methods of vocabulary instruction. *Journal of Reading, 29,* 596–602.

Harp, B., & Brewer, J. (2005) *The informed reading teacher: Research-based practice.* Upper Saddle River, N.J.: Pearson.

Nagy, W. I., & Herman, P. A. (1987) Breadth and depth of vocabulary knowledge: Implications for acquisition and instruction. In M. G. McKeown & M. E. Curtis (Eds.), *The nature of vocabulary acquisition* (19–35). Hillsdale, N.J.: Lawrence Erlbaum.

Watts, S. (1995) Vocabulary instruction during reading lessons in six classrooms. *Journal of Reading Behavior, 27,* 399–424.

COMPREHENSION SKILLS

R eading is the act of creating meaning with text. This chapter describes how to improve students' ability to comprehend expository text through the use of comprehension skills.

Types of Text

As adults living and reading in the real world we read a lot of different types of text. The two main types of text are expository text (informational text like this textbook) and narrative text or stories. However, each of these has a different purpose and should be approached differently (Zarillo, 1991).

Narrative Text

We read narrative text (stories) for the same reason we watch movies: to be entertained and to enjoy the story. Could you imagine seeing a really great movie, only to have somebody demand that you write a movie report to prove that you'd actually seen it? How would you react if you were required to fill out a comprehension worksheet to demonstrate your ability to comprehend the movie? How might you feel if somebody demanded that you recount movie details and identify the plot, climax, and resolution? Yet these are the types of postreading experiences that are common (Allington, 1994). And what do they accomplish? They make reading less pleasurable and keep students from entering the world of the book. They also make it far less likely that students will fall in love with books.

Instead, we want our postreading activities and conversations for narrative text to reflect the types of conversation we might have after seeing a really great movie. Questions and activities for stories should reflect an aesthetic response (described in the next chapter) and not simply be used to have students regurgitate story details (Rosenblatt, 1983).

Expository Text

We read expository texts in order to get information and ideas from them. Although I'd like to think that my writing is so interesting that you'd read it on the beach during your summer vacation, I realize that most of you are reading this book to get information. As such, you approach the reading of this informational textbook much differently than you would approach a Harry Potter book.

The point then is this: Comprehension skills should be used with expository text to help students retrieve information and construct meaning. However, they should not be used with narrative text. But what if students are not able to comprehend the story that they're reading? Find them a story they can comprehend. Reading is a pleasurable act. Just as we probably wouldn't sit through a movie we didn't enjoy or couldn't comprehend, we should not force students to slog through books that bore or confuse them.

Comprehension Skills

In most classrooms today very little time is spent teaching students how to comprehend expository text (Reutzel & Cooter, 1996). Instead, the majority of time is spent on word identification skills and oral reading fluency. We expect students to be able to read their textbooks, but we don't teach them how to do it. It doesn't take a genius to understand that students need explicit instruction in the use of comprehension skills in order to comprehend expository text effectively (Guthrie et al., 1996).

Let's start with a definition: Comprehension skills are strategies readers use to retrieve information and construct meaning from expository text. They are the thinking processes, broken down into steps, that are used to comprehend. These must be taught explicitly (see below). Three types of comprehension skills are described below: prereading, during-reading, and postreading. These comprehension skills can be easily learned and flexibly applied to a variety of reading situations.

Prereading Comprehension Skills

Prereading comprehension skills are used primarily to preview the structure of the text to be read or to connect new information to knowledge readers might already know. Three prereading comprehension skills are presented here:

Preview/Overview

1. Look at the title and headings.

2. Read the first and last paragraphs.

3. Read the article/chapter.

Web and Brainstorm

1. Look at the title and headings.

2. Create a web with a central node and subnodes.

3. Brainstorm on each subnode.

4. Read the article/chapter.

5. Add to and modify the original web as (or after) you read.

Outline and Brainstorm

1. Look at the title and headings.

2. Create an outline with title and headings.

3. Brainstorm on each heading.

4. Read the article/chapter.

5. Add to and modify the original outline as (or after) you read.

Preview and Overview.   Using this skill, the reader first notes the title and headings in the text to get a sense of the structure. Next, the first and final paragraphs are read to get a sense of the content. This helps the reader interpret the text as it is then read. Finally, the text or chapter is read.

If there are no headings, students simply note the title and read the first and last paragraph. The Preview-O-Graph below can be used to provide structure and to keep students actively engaged as they learn this skill. Here students read the first paragraph and the last paragraph and list one to three ideas from each. Next, they list three to eight things they already know about the topic to be read. This helps them connect new information to knowledge they already have. To get these known ideas, students should brainstorm with a partner, in small group, or large group (more knowledge from which to draw). For example, if students were reading a chapter on life jackets, you would ask, "What are some things you already know about life jackets?" Finally, important information from the text is recorded. Experiment with this. Some students prefer to record information from the text as they're reading; others prefer to read the entire chapter or article and then go back and record the interesting or important ideas.

Preview-O-Graph
First Paragraph
1.
2.
3.

What I Know
1.
2.
3.
4.
5.

Last Paragraph

1.

2.

3.

Information from the Text

1.

2.

3.

Web and Brainstorm. Here the structure of the text is used to create a semantic web. You could use an outline to get the same effect as a web; however, because it is more visual, some students prefer the web to an outline. To use this, first put the title or topic of the chapter or text in a center circle. Next, the headings of each section are then used to create nodes. Then, brainstorm on each node to generate relevant knowledge (see figure 13.1). The web provides a graphic organizer that shows the relationship between concepts. These are then used to help the reader interpret the text. Finally, read the text.

This same web can also be used as a during- or postreading activity. Here, a web is created using just the topic and headings. As they are reading or after reading, use the information from the text to add to the web.

Outline and Brainstorm. The brainstorm is the same as the web and brainstorm except it uses outline form (see below). Again, some students prefer this form to the web. You should teach and demonstrate how to use both, then allow students to choose the one that works best for them. As with the web, the outline can also be used as a during- or postreading activity.

Life Jackets

I. Certified

1.

2.

II. Waterskiing

1.

2.

III. Young Children

1.

2.

Web and Brainstorm for Pre-Reading

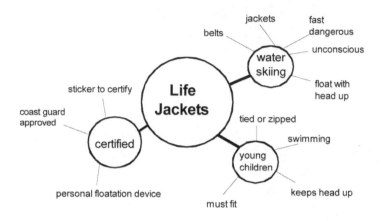

Web and Brainstorm for During- and Post-Reading

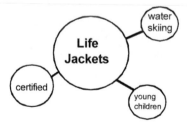

Figure 13.1.   Web and Brainstorming for Pre-, During-, and Post-comprehension Skills

During-Reading Comprehension Skills

During-reading comprehension skills are used to monitor comprehension, to evaluate ideas gleaned from each paragraph, and to begin to organize ideas within the structure of the text as students are reading. Two during-reading comprehension skills are presented here:

Paragraph Reread

1. Read each paragraph quickly.

2. Reread to find important sentences or ideas.

3. Continue.

Read and Pause

1. Read a paragraph.

2. Pause and check. (Do I understand?)

3. Return or resume.

Paragraph Reread. This skill is used intuitively by many expert readers. First, a paragraph is read quickly to get a general sense of its content. Next, the paragraph is read a second time. Finally, the reader identifies important ideas and continues. This also helps the reader to make connections with the other ideas found in the text.

The Paragraph-O-Graph can be used as a graphic organizer to teach this skill. In the column on the left, students record paragraph ideas from the text. The column on the right is used for their interpretations, analysis, or associations. This is a way for students to connect their own personal knowledge and experience to what they are reading. These ideas can be added as students are reading or after, as a postreading activity. Again, invite students to experiment to find the method that works best for them. (Our brains all work differently. There is no such thing as the best method for comprehending expository text.)

Paragraph-O-Graph

Paragraph Ideas	**Your Ideas**
1. Many types of life jackets.	1. I didn't know there were so many kinds of life jackets. I only used them on a lake.
2. Must be coast guard certified.	2. I can see why this is so important. This could mean the difference between life and death. Can you image what would happen if a life jacket didn't float? It would become a death jacket.
3. Waterskiing, head must float.	3. When I used to water-ski, I just used a life belt. This would have kept my body above water, but not my head.

Read and Pause. This skill is designed primarily to help students monitor their comprehension as they're reading. While expert readers do this spontaneously, beginning readers need to be taught. Here readers pause after each paragraph to see if there is sufficient understanding, then they either return to reread the paragraph or continue reading the next paragraph. Some readers find it helpful to use a 3x5 index card to help them focus and concentrate when reading. The card is moved to the bottom of each paragraph as it is being read. This keeps their eyes from moving ahead until they have monitored their comprehension.

Postreading Comprehension Skill

Postreading skills are used to reconstruct important ideas, organize those ideas, and evaluate those ideas after reading a chapter or article. Two postreading comprehension skills are presented here:

Article Reread

1. Read the article/chapter quickly.

2. Reread the article/chapter.

3. Note or record important ideas.

Webbing and Outlining

1. Read the chapter/text quickly.

2. Create web or outline.

3. Create web or outline based on headings or content.

4. Reread chapter/text.

5. Record interesting or important ideas in web/outline.

Article Reread. First, the text is read quickly to provide the reader with a sense of topic. Then, this knowledge is used to interpret, sort, and evaluate the information as the text is read a second time. Finally, interesting or important ideas are recorded (students take notes as they read the chapter or article the second time).

Webbing and Outlining. As described above, webbing and outlining can both be used as postreading comprehension skills. Here the reader reads the article through once very quickly to get a sense of the content. An outline or web is created based on the content. The reader then reads the chapter or article a second time. Interesting or important ideas are recorded in the appropriate place in the web or outline.

Teaching Comprehension Skills

We cannot assume, at any age or level, that students know how to read expository text. Explicit instruction must be used to teach them how to use comprehension skills. The five elements of effective skills instruction should be used here: (a) direct instruction and modeling, (b) identification of the procedural components, (c) guided practice, (d) regular practice, and (e) application or use in other areas in order to ensure transfer (Pressley, Harris, & Marks, 1992).

Direct instruction and modeling. First, select a comprehension skill to teach. Introduce it by telling students it's a way to help them understand what they read when reading informational text. Then, explain how it should be used. To do this, read a short piece of text out loud. Make your thought process transparent by thinking out loud (cognitive modeling) in order to demonstrate exactly how the comprehension skill is used. This element provides an overview and should be relatively brief. Example:

> **Mr. Jackson:** "Comprehension skills help us to understand what we read. They're used when we're trying to get information from a text. Today we're going to learn a comprehension skill called Read and Pause. This skill will help you understand your textbooks and other informational text.
>
> "Listen to me as I use this skill." (*Here, Mr. Jackson reads one paragraph of the text out loud, then pauses.*) "Let's see . . . I've read the paragraph, and now I'm going to pause to see if I really understood what I was reading." (*Mr. Jackson pauses.*)
>
> "I feel a little confused, so I'm going to go back and read the paragraph a second time." (*Mr. Jackson reads the paragraph out loud a second time.*)

Identification of the steps or parts. This element is often intertwined with direct instruction and modeling. Here, you identify the specific steps used with the comprehension skill. It's helpful to use a thinking frame to teach these steps. A thinking frame is the steps of any thinking process, broken down into specific steps. Below you can see the thinking frame for Read and Pause. This is used to support the thought process as students begin to learn a new type of thinking (Johnson, 1996). Thinking frames can be constructed in poster form and placed in the classroom for effective teaching and easy review. Here's an example of Mr. Jackson identifying the steps used in this comprehension skill:

> **Mr. Jackson:** (*Mr. Jackson points to a poster placed in front of the room with the three comprehension skills on it.*) "The steps of Read and Pause are:
>
> **Read and Pause**
> 1. Read a paragraph.
> 2. Pause and check. (Do I understand?)
> 3. Return or resume.
> "In this case, I didn't quite understand what I just read, so I returned and read the paragraph again. I find that this helped me to get a better idea of what I was reading. You should do this after you read each paragraph."

Guided practice. Guided practice, sometimes referred to as scaffolded instruction, is provided when the teacher takes the whole class through each step of the skill (Johnson & Graves, 1997). The goal here is to provide the support necessary to allow students to learn to use the skill independently. To teach a comprehension skill, the teacher (a) teaches the steps of the comprehension skill initially; (b) takes the whole class through each step of the skill several times; and (c) designs an activity so that students can practice the skill independently. Below, Mr. Jackson uses guided practice to teach this comprehension skill:

Mr. Jackson: "Let's try one together." (*All students have a similar copy of a short expository text consisting of five paragraphs.*) "Read the next paragraph silently to yourself. Pause when you have finished." (*All students read. When the majority of students have finished, Mr. Jackson continues.*)

"Sometimes, if we read something we're not familiar with, it's hard to understand it the first time. Let's see how well the information sank in." (*Mr. Jackson calls on a few students to provide important ideas from the paragraph. If the ideas seem to be off the mark he will ask students to reread it. If students seem to have grasped the important ideas, they will resume reading. He does this with each paragraph until the article is completed.*)

Regular practice and review. Like any skill, students need regular practice and review in order to be able to use comprehension skills effectively. Any time students are asked to read expository text, they should be reminded to use a comprehension skill. This is where thinking frames can be used to quickly point to the steps and encourage students to select and use a comprehension skill with which they are comfortable. Here is an example of how Mr. Jackson uses regular practice and review:

Mr. Jackson: (*The next day in science class.*) "Before we begin our science lesson, we're going to quickly practice using the comprehension skill we learned yesterday, Read and Pause." (*Each student opens the text to the chapter that will be assigned that day.*)

"With this comprehension skill, you read a paragraph, pause to see if you've understood what you've just read, and then either return and reread the paragraph or resume reading. Go ahead and try this with the first three paragraphs. When you're finished, record two or three ideas in your reading journal that you think are interesting or important. Be ready to share these." (*Mr. Jackson allows time for most of the students to read the text and record some ideas, then he continues.*)

"Were there any paragraphs that you needed to read only once? What paragraphs did you have to read twice? Who has an idea from the text that they're ready to share?"

Integration into the curriculum. Comprehension skills should be used throughout the curriculum at all levels whenever students are asked to read expository text. Students of all ages and at all levels should be reminded of the steps necessary to successfully comprehend a piece of expository text before beginning to read an assigned chapter or article. Using comprehension skills this way provides students with additional comprehension practice as well as helps them to more effectively construct meaning with assigned texts. Here is an example of Mr. Jackson integrating comprehension skills into his curriculum:

Mr. Jackson: (*Mr. Jackson has just finished describing the solar system to his fifth-grade students. Now, he wants them to read the chapter in the science textbook that reinforces the concepts he covered in his lesson. He points to the chart that has the thinking frame for Read and Pause located on the wall near the front of the room.*) "For tomorrow, you'll be reading chapter 5: 'The Solar System.' You have about thirty minutes in class today to start. That should be time for many of you to finish. Try using our new comprehension skill, Read and Pause, to help you get the ideas from this chapter. Remember the steps." (*Again, he points to the poster and quickly reviews each step.*)

"When you're finished reading this chapter, record four ideas you think are interesting or important and be ready to share with your group."

Final Word

This chapter described comprehension skills and demonstrated how they can be taught most effectively. In the next three chapters, you will find a wealth of strategies and activities that teachers can use with both narrative and expository texts to enhance comprehension and to make the reading experience more interesting and enjoyable.

Internet Search Terms

Comprehension skills: *comprehension-skills, reading-comprehension-skills, teaching-comprehension-skills, learning-reading-comprehension-skills.*

Comprehension: *enhancing-comprehension, enhancing-reading-comprehension, strategies-enhancing-reading-comprehension, strategies-comprehension, strategies-reading, research-comprehension.*

Effective skills instruction: *elements-effective-skills-instruction, effective-skills-instruction, teaching-reading-skills, direct-instruction, Michael-Pressley-skills-instruction, how-to-teach-a-skill.*

References

Allington, R. L. (1994) The schools we have. The schools we need. *The Reading Teacher, 48*, 13–29.

Guthrie, J., Van Meter, P., McCann, A., Wigfield, A., Bennet, L., Poundstone, C., Rice, M., Failbisch, F., Hunt, B., & Mitchell, A. (1996) Growth of literacy engagement: Changes in motivations and skills during concept-oriented reading instruction. *Reading Research Quarterly, 31*, 306–32.

Johnson, A. (1996) Inference: A thinking skill to enhance learning and literacy. *Wisconsin State Reading Association Journal, 40*, 19–24.

Johnson, A., & Graves, M. (1997) Scaffolding: A tool for enhancing the reading experiences of all students. *Texas Journal of Reading, 3*, 31–37.

Pressley, M., Harris, K. R., & Marks, M. B. (1992) But good skill users are constructivists! *Educational Psychology Review, 4*, 3–31.

Reutzel, D. R., & Cooter, R. B. (1996) *Teaching children to read.* Englewood Cliffs, N.J.: Merrill/Prentice Hall.

Rosenblatt, L. M. (1983) *Literature as exploration* (fourth ed.). New York: Modern Language Association.

Zarillo, J. (1991) Theory becomes practice: Aesthetic teaching with literature. *The New Advocate, 4*, 221–34.

STRATEGIES FOR NARRATIVE TEXT

The last chapter described comprehension skills that should be explicitly taught to students to enable them to understand expository text. These next two chapters describe a variety of strategies and activities that can be used with narrative text. These are all designed to get students to interact with story ideas and to make connections with literature, which, in turn, will enhance comprehension. These strategies and activities can also be the basis for literature log entries as well as other types of assignments and activities.

Activities to Encourage Interaction with Narrative Text

Rating Character Traits

This is a postreading activity where students identify three or four character traits and then rate the degree to which various characters in the story display those traits (see figure 14.1). Eventually students will be able to select their own characters and traits to rate. This activity invites students to go beyond the written text, to infer, and to look for clues to support their rating. Students can also rate and compare characters from different stories, from real life, history, current events, or even their own lives. It can be an effective way to make connections with literature. Results can be displayed in a journal or on a poster in either table or graph form.

Table for Rating Character Traits

	Brave	Smart	Strong	Friendly
Dorothy	8	7	8	10
Luke Skywalker	9	8	9	9
Don Rumsfeld	1	1	1	1
Neo	7	7	9	5
Martin Luther King	9	9	7	8
Andy Johnson	7	9	9	5

Key: 10 = very high; 5 = average; 1 = very low

Graph for Rating Character Traits

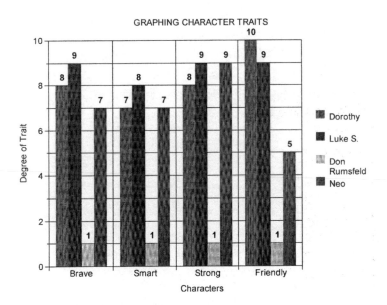

Figure 14.1. Rating Character Traits

Character Maps

Character maps are a postreading activity in which students identify two or three describing adjectives for a story character and then find supporting details. First draw a circle in the middle of a sheet of paper with the name of a story character on it. Next, find two to three character traits

CHARACTER MAP

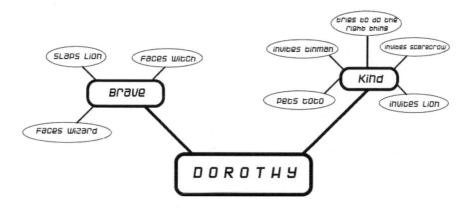

Figure 14.2.   Character Maps

or adjectives that are descriptive of that character. These become nodes. Then, list story events that reflect or indicate each of the describing adjectives (see figure 14.2). To make the personal connection, students would then create a character map of themselves, a friend, or a person they admire.

Person Chart

The person chart is a postreading activity that invites students to use story details to make inferences about what a character might like and dislike, as well as things they are good at and not good at (see figure 14.3).

Double Journal Entry

A double journal entry combines objective story details with students' subjective analysis (below). Draw a line down the center of a journal page. In the column on the left, students record the exact details from the text. This could be a passage copied verbatim or a description of what happened. In the column on the right students record their ideas, analysis, interpretations, or associations with the things in the other column.

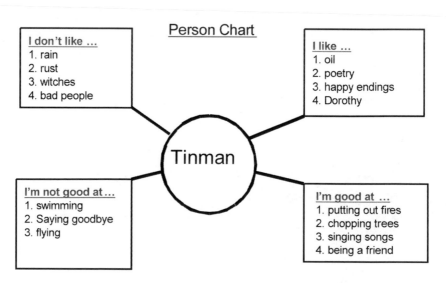

Person Chart

I don't like ...
1. rain
2. rust
3. witches
4. bad people

I like ...
1. oil
2. poetry
3. happy endings
4. Dorothy

Tinman

I'm not good at...
1. swimming
2. Saying goodbye
3. flying

I'm good at ...
1. putting out fires
2. chopping trees
3. singing songs
4. being a friend

Figure 14.3.   Person Chart

Double Journal Entry

Text	**My Ideas**
Dorothy: No—it was an accident. I didn't mean to kill anybody; really, I didn't.	The Witch, green face, scrunched up. Everyone is scared. The Witch represents the shadow side, that part of us that we all have inside.
Witch: You didn't, eh? Accident, eh? Well, I can cause accidents too, my little pretty, and this is how I do it . . .	
Uncle Henry tells Dorothy that he won't let Miss Gulch take Toto. Miss Gulch tells him that he could lose the farm as a result. Uncle Henry takes Toto from a sobbing Dorothy and puts him in Miss Gulch's basket.	Apparently Uncle Henry doesn't have the moral fiber that Dorothy has. He takes a moral stand, but then changes his mind. He is willing to have Toto destroyed. What kind of spineless weasel is Uncle Henry?

Comparing T-Chart

A comparing T-chart is simple a way to compare any two characters, items, story events, chapters, or stories side by side. The first comparing T-chart in figure 14.4 enables the reader to make very personal connections to the story. The second T-chart enables the reader to make connections with other stories (a movie story).

Compare-O-Graph

The compare-o-graph enables students to compare many characters (or other things) simultaneously. By including myself in the compare-o-graph in figure 14.5, I am able to make personal connections with the story.

Attribute Chart

The attribute chart is similar to the compare-o-graph; however, it specifies the attributes up front. Again, you can use this to compare (a) stories found in different chapters, books, movies, or TV shows; (b) characters from the stories, TV, movies, real life, history, or current events; or events from stories, real life, or history. The attribute chart in figure 14.6 is used to compare different characters or people.

My bad day	Dorothy's bad day
got up late	Fell in the pig pen
cornflakes were soggy	Nobody wants to listen to her
got yelled at on the bus	Crabby lady tries to take her dog
lost my homework	Tornado comes
got teased at recess	Gets hit on the head by a window
dropped the ball in gym	A witch tries to kill her

Ideas/Conclusions: Both Dorothy and I had bad days. Her day was much worse than mine.

Luke Skywalker	Dorothy
Orphan	Orphan
Bad person tried to kill him.	Bad person tried to kill her
Lives in the future	Lives in the past
Gets instruction from wise teacher	Has a dog
Has a sister	Wears a dress

Ideas/Conclusions: Dorothy and Luke Skywalker share many similar traits.

Figure 14.4. Comparing T-Charts

Comparison Chart

The comparison chart is a graphic organizer that can be used for comparing and contrasting any two things, characters, events, books, stories (figure 14.7). It is similar to the Venn diagram but is actually easier as it provides more structure. When comparing and contrasting, start with similarities. These are listed in the middle column. Then list differences in the outer columns. Comparing and contrasting is a high level thinking

COMPARE–O–GRAPH			
Me	**Dorothy**	**Luke Skywalker**	**Arthur**
No sister	No sister	Has a sister	Has a sister
Written word	Magic slippers	Light saber	Sword
Very handsome	Very beautiful	Okay	Don't know
Can sing	Can sing	Don't know	Don't know
Ideas/Conclusions:			

Figure 14.5. Compare-O-Graph

ATTRIBUTE CHART					
	Can Sing	Can dance	Loves honey	Battles evil	Battles paparazzi
Me	x		x	x	x
Dorothy	x	x		x	
Luke Skywalker				x	
Winnie-the-Pooh			x		
Britney Spears	x	x			x
Ideas/Conclusions:					

Figure 14.6. Attribute Chart

skill (Johnson, 2000). The graphic organizer provides structure for students' thinking as they learn how to do this.

Story Analysis

Story analysis is another high level thinking process that can be used as a postreading activity. Here students have to analyze the story (or chapter) and decide what the beginning, middle, and ending parts of the story are, and which parts go in each. A simple story analysis chart can be used to organize their thinking (below).

COMPARISON CHART

Dorothy Gale	↓ Similarities ↓	Luke Skywalker
female	• didn't know parents	male
evil form is female	• friends to help	evil form is male
earth	• gain special powers	space
past	• battles evil	future
wise sage is female	• evil portrayed as dark or black	wise sage is male

↑
Differences

↑
Differences

Figure 14.7. Comparison Chart

Analyzing Story Parts

List interesting or important events that occurred in each part of the story:

Beginning
- In Kansas
- Miss Gulch takes dog
- Dorothy runs away
- Tornado comes
- Dorothy gets carried to Oz
- House lands on Witch

Middle
- Finds herself in Oz
- Meets Glinda and Wicked Witch
- Tries to find the Wizard to get home
- Meets Tinman, Scarecrow, and Lion

End
- Kills Witch
- Brings broom to Wizard
- Gets in balloon
- Shoes take her home
- Says she'll never leave home again

Story Map

A story map is any visual representation of the story plot. It's a map that lays out the story events so that you can see them in order. Story maps come in a variety for forms (see Internet search terms at the end of this chapter). Time lines are the simplest form of a story map. The first story map in figure 14.8 can be used as a prereading activity. Here the teacher

Pre-reading Story Map

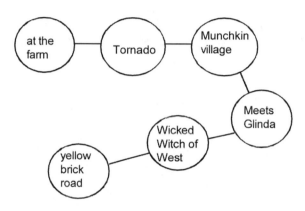

During- or Post-Reading Story Map

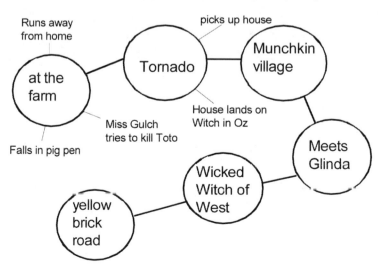

Figure 14.8a. Story Maps

Literal Story Map

Figure 14.8b.   Story Map

creates a visual representation of the major events or elements in a book or chapter. This provides structure and a preview/overview to enhance students' comprehension as they read the story independently. It can then be used as a during- or postreading activity. Here students would list interesting or important events related to each of the nodes or bubbles. Finally, a story map can be a literal map of where the story took place. The literal story map calls for students to use inference, story clues, and their creativity to imagine the actual physical space in which the story took place.

Story maps are open-ended activities in which students at all levels can experience some level of success. Eventually students will be able to design and create their own story maps. Story maps also provide a good sense of how students comprehend and interpret story events, and as such, can be used as a replacement for comprehension worksheets.

Story Grammar

Just as sentences have a certain grammatical structure (nouns, verbs, and the like), stories too have a structure (characters, setting, a problem, and a solution/resolution) that is called story grammar. Understanding story grammar enhances students' ability to comprehend narrative text. Story grammar can also be used as a prereading activity. Here important characters, the setting, and one or more problems are introduced. Students are then asked to read to find out how the problem is resolved. Story grammar can also be used to provide structure for students doing book talks (see chapter 6). Here is an example of story grammar for *The Wizard of Oz*:

Story Grammar (a type of story map)
Important characters:
1. Dorothy.
2. Glinda.
3. Witch.
4. Lion.
5. Scarecrow.
6. Tinman.
7. Wizard.
Where/when:
1. Kansas.
2. Oz.
Problem:
1. Dorothy wants to get home.
2. Brain, heart, and courage for others.
3. Witch.
Solution:
1. Melts Witch.
2. Taps shoes to get home.
Things that happened:
1. Tornado lifted house to Oz.
2. Kidnapped by Witch.
3. Visited Wizard.
4. Fell asleep in field of poppies.

CHAPTER FOURTEEN

Orderizer

This postreading activity asks students to put things in order based on a variety of criteria (not simply chronological order). Below are some of the criteria that can be used for putting events, characters, or things found in stories in order (you're limited only by your imagination):

- Most important to least
- Chronologically
- Most like you to least like you
- Funny to not funny
- Real to unreal
- Expensive to cheap
- Interesting to boring
- Happy to sad
- Good to evil
- Wise to silly
- Healthy to unhealthy
- Magical to ordinary
- Friendly to mean
- Practical to impractical
- Dangerous to safe
- Imaginative to unimaginative
- Innovative to ordinary
- Dark to light
- Near to far
- Old to new
- Most expensive to least expensive

- Big to little

- Good decision to poor decision

- Pragmatic to nonsensical

- Nice to not nice

- Wide to skinny

The Orderizer is a graphic organizer that can be used to guide students' thinking during this process. First, list four to eight items, characters, or events in the column on the left. Then look at the criteria. Finally, arrange items, characters, or events in order according to the criteria. As you see below, the same events, characters, or things can be arranged differently according to the criteria.

Orderizer
CRITERION: CHRONOLOGY

Events	In Order
1. Oils Tinman.	1. Dorothy runs away from home.
2. Gives Witch's broomstick to Oz.	2. Oils Tinman.
3. Finds a little man behind the curtain.	3. Dorothy slaps lion.
4. Dorothy slaps lion.	4. Gives Witch's broomstick to Oz.
5. Dorothy runs away from home.	5. Finds a little man behind the curtain.

CRITERION: HAPPY THINGS

Events	In Order
1. Oils Tinman.	1. Oils Tinman.
2. Gives Witch's broomstick to Oz.	2. Gives Witch's broomstick to Oz.
3. Finds a little man behind the curtain.	3. Finds a little man behind the curtain.
4. Dorothy slaps lion.	4. Dorothy slaps lion.
5. Dorothy runs away from home.	5. Dorothy runs away from home.

CRITERION: IMPORTANCE

Events	In Order
1. Oils Tinman.	1. Finds a little man behind the curtain.
2. Gives Witch's broomstick to Oz.	2. Gives Witch's broomstick to Oz.
3. Finds a little man behind the curtain.	3. Oils Tinman.
4. Dorothy slaps lion.	4. Dorothy runs away from home.
5. Dorothy runs away from home.	5. Dorothy slaps lion.

CRITERION: IMPORTANCE

Objects	In Order
1. Basket.	1. Ruby red slippers.
2. Broomstick.	2. Broomstick.
3. Ruby red slippers.	3. Balloon.
4. Balloon.	4. Oil can.
5. Oil can.	5. Basket.

CRITERION: BIG to LITTLE

Objects	In Order
1. Basket.	1. Oil can.
2. Broomstick.	2. Ruby red slippers.
3. Ruby red slippers.	3. Basket.
4. Balloon.	4. Broomstick.
5. Oil can.	5. Balloon.

CRITERION: BIG to LITTLE

Characters	In Order
1. Dorothy.	1. Lion.
2. Mayor.	2. Auntie Em.
3. Flying monkey.	3. Dorothy.
4. Auntie Em.	4. Mayor.
5. Lion.	5. Flying monkey.

This postreading activity provides a good sense of how students comprehend and interpret story events. Also, it's open-ended so that all students can experience some level of success. It can be done individually, with students recording their ideas in a journal or reading log. It can also be done in small group in which students create posters to hang on the wall or bulletin board. It's worth noting that the conversation that takes place as students work in groups is much more important than the product they come up with. As students discuss, disagree, and try to make their case, they use story details to support their decisions.

The Orderizer can also be used with expository text and it can be used to put order to any factors, people, or events across the curriculum, in current events, history, or in students' lives. For example:

1. What are five things that happened this week in the world? Arrange them in order of importance.

2. What are five things that happened this week in your life? Arrange them in order of interesting to boring.

3. What are five things that happened in your life? Arrange them from happy to sad.

4. What are five things that have happened in the world this year? Arrange them chronologically.

5. Who are five people you have interacted with this week? Arrange them in order of friendly to not friendly.

6. What are five important physical things in our community? Arrange them in order of most important to least important.

Plot Profile

The plot profile can be used with individual chapters or with complete books. Students begin by recording interesting or important events that occurred. These are then put in chronological order and numbered. The numbers corresponding to each event are listed on the horizontal axis on the bottom of a line graph (see figure 14.9). The vertical axis is numbered from 1 to 10 and is used to rate-sort some criteria (happy or sad, exciting or boring, good or bad, or important or not important). Each story event is then rated. Each point is connected with a line to show change over time.

To extend, ask students to list interesting or important events in their lives, in the past year, the past week, or the day. They can also list current events, historical events, school/classroom events, or community events. A similar axis and rating system is then used to show change over time. Plot profiles can be shared with a buddy or in a small group or using a large poster. They can be done individually, with a partner, or in small group. Again, when working in small groups, the actual product students create is not nearly as important as the thinking and discussion that takes place in creating it.

Plot Profile for Story Events

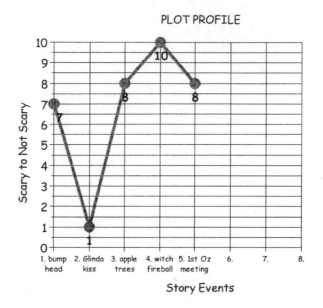

Plot Profile for Students' Life Events

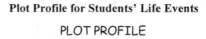

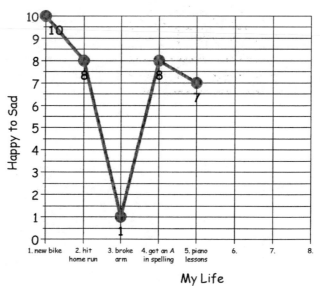

Figure 14.9.   Plot Profiles

Internet Search Terms

Story maps: *story-map-reading, story-map, story-map-literature, graphic-organizer-reading, graphic-organizer-literature, character-map-reading, timeline-reading, time-line-reading.*

Postreading activities: *postreading-activities, post-reading-activities, developing-reading-activities, reader-response-activities, aesthetic-response-activities, plot-profile, literature-activities, attribute-chart-reading, attribute-chart-post-reading.*

References

Johnson, A. (2000) *Up and out: Using thinking skills to enhance learning.* Needham Heights, Mass.: Allyn and Bacon.

MORE STRATEGIES FOR NARRATIVE TEXT

This chapter describes ten more strategies for narrative text that can be used to get students to make personal connections with the story, to think deeper and in more complex ways about story elements, and to enhance comprehension. As with all strategies in this book, they should be adopted and adapted to meet your particular teaching needs and situation.

Additional Activities to Encourage Interaction with Narrative Text

Cause-Effect-O-Graph
The cause-effect-o-graph is a graphic organizer to help students identify cause and effect. Given a cause, students must find or infer the possible effect. Or given the effect, students must find or infer the possible cause. It can be used as both a prereading and a postreading activity with both narrative and expository text. As a prereading activity, tell students briefly about the upcoming selection, then provide them with a purposeful question: "In this chapter, Dorothy runs away from home (effect). Let's read to see if we can find what causes her to do this." You could also provide the cause and see if they can predict or infer the effect: "In this chapter, the witch throws a fireball at Scarecrow. What do you think will happen?"

Cause-Effect-O-Graph

CAUSE	EFFECT
1. _____.➜	1. Dorothy ran away from home.
2. Dorothy woke up in Kansas. ➜	2. _____.
3. _____.➜	3. Tinman was rusted in place.
4. Dorothy stayed in Oz. ➜	4. _____.
5. _____.➜	5. Lion cries.
6. Witch throws fireball at Scarecrow. ➜	6. _____.

As a postreading activity, the cause-effect-o-graph can be used to identify literal answers that are found in the text or inferential or imaginative answers. An example of a literal answer above would be effect #3: Tinman was rusted in place. There is a specific text-based answer for this that students would need to find. An example of an inferential or imaginative answer above would be cause #4: Dorothy stayed in Oz. "Boys and girls, what do you think would happen back on the farm in Kansas if Dorothy decided to stay in Oz? What might have happened in Oz?"

Head Chart

A head chart is used to get inside the head of different story characters in order to analyze their reactions to similar events or to imagine and infer what they might be thinking. After reading a story, three or four story events are listed in the Events column on the left of the head chart. Two to four story characters are listed horizontally along the top of the chart. Students are then asked to describe each character's reaction to each of the events, or to imagine what they might be thinking.

A natural extension would be to use the head chart to create dialogue, short dramatic performances, and reader's theater productions. This activity could also be extended by using real-life events found in history, the news, or students' lives.

Head Chart
Event—House falls on Witch of the East.
Dorothy: I'm confused. I didn't mean to hurt anybody. Now they're calling me a killer?
Witch: Where are the slippers? I want them! I want power.

Munchkin Mayor: My goodness, I hope nobody hurts us. Dorothy must be very powerful.

Event—Glinda appears in Munchkinland.
Dorothy: Who is this beautiful person? Why does she talk funny?
Witch: I hate her. I'm mad. She's always messing with me.
Munchkin Mayor: Glinda! Hurray! She always helps and protects us.

Event—Dorothy sets off to Oz.
Dorothy: I hope I can find this Wizard. I want to go home.
Witch: I'll need to find a way to get this girl so that I can have her shoes. I want power!
Munchkin Mayor: What a nice young lady this Dorothy is. I sure hope she makes it to Oz. I wonder, what's for lunch?

Head Connector

Related to the head chart above, the head connector is used to get inside the head of a story character as he or she reacts to a story event and then to find a connection to students' lives. Students here must make a personal connection to the story by identifying a similar feeling, event, or situation. These ideas are best shared in small groups.

Head Connector

Story Event—Lion jumps out of the bushes and starts growling at Toto, tries to pick a fight with Tinman and Scarecrow.
Dorothy: I'm angry. It's not fair to see somebody bigger picking on somebody smaller. Poor Toto couldn't defend himself against a big Lion. I'm so angry, I'm going to slap that lion on the nose.
My life: I was angry. I was at a movie. Four teenagers in front of me were text messaging with their phones. It made it hard to concentrate on the movie. It was very selfish and inconsiderate. I asked the four kids (not very nicely) to put their phones away. I think I growled at them.

Ranking Decisions

Ranking decisions is a postreading activity that invites students to make personal connections with a story by generating alternative decisions and ranking them in order. First, identify a situation in the story in which a decision must be made. Then, in small groups or large group, ask students to generate three to four possible decisions that could be made. Students then rank the decisions based on what they think is best.

> **Ranking Decisions**
> Situation: Miss Gulch wants to take Toto and have him destroyed.
> **POSSIBLE DECISIONS**
> Run away from home.
> Get to know Miss Gulch. Try to reason with her. Offer to help her at home.
> Send Toto away to live with somebody else.
> Threaten Miss Gulch. Be mean to her.
> Be kind to Miss Gulch. Offer to work in her garden.
> Talk with the humane society. See if they can help.
> **RANK IN ORDER OF PREFERENCE**
> 1. Get to know Miss Gulch. Try to reason with her. Offer to help her at home.
> 2. Be kind to Miss Gulch. Offer to work in her garden.
> 3. Talk with the humane society. See if they can help.
> 4. Send Toto away to live with somebody else.
> 5. Run away from home.
> 6. Threaten Miss Gulch. Be mean to her.

Adjective Fun

Three activities using adjectives are described below. With some imagination and tweaking, they can also be used with nouns, verbs, pronouns, and other grammatical elements.

Ordering adjectives. Students identify some or all of the adjectives found in a chapter or a book. In their journal they arrange them according to those that are most like them to those that are least like them. Use no more than three to six adjectives with younger students, five to ten with older students.

Describing adjectives. Students look for one to five story adjectives in the story that describe their day, their week, or their lives. In their journals, they list the adjective(s) and describe the connection.

Adjectives of our lives. Students are given one or more adjectives from the story. In their journals they then describe various events or moments in their lives that are related to each adjective.

Predict-O-Graph

Predicting is another skill that good readers do naturally as they are reading. A prediction is a guess related to a future event based on clues. The key to teaching students how to predict is to get them to first identify story clues instead of just guessing. The predict-o-graph below can be used to help students organize their thinking here. The advanced predict-o-graph uses information in the text combined with information students know. These can be used a pre-, during-, or postreading activity. They can also be used to make predictions across the curriculum, in current events, or in students' lives.

Predict-O-Graph
What will happen next?

<u>Clues</u>
1.
2.
3.
4.

Prediction:

Advanced Predict-O-Graph

1. Read/listen to the selection.
2. Write down important information in the column on the left.
3. Write down information you know related to the prediction in the column on the right.
4. Looking at the information above, predict what you think will happen next.

What will happen next?

Information from the text:

Information I know (from my head):

Infer-O-Graph

Like making predictions, good readers also make inferences. They go beyond the descriptions found in the story or text to fill in some of the story details as they are reading. They try to understand ideas not explicitly stated in the text. Like the prediction above, an inference is not simply a guess. It's a conclusion based on information that is already known. The infer-o-graph below organizes students' thinking as they learn this skill. This can be used as a postreading activity. It can also be used to make inferences across the curriculum, in current events, or in students' lives.

> Infer-O-Graph
> *Inference question:* What kind of person was Professor Marvel?
> **Text Clues**
> 1. Shared a hot dog with Toto.
> 2. Tried to get Dorothy to go back home.
> 3. Dropped by at the end of the movie to see if Dorothy was all right.
> 4. Volunteers to answer Dorothy's questions.
>
> *Inference:* Professor Marvel was basically a kind person.

Aesthetic Response Questions and Activities

As we read in chapter 13, the purpose for reading stories is to be entertained and to enjoy them. Thus, postreading questions and activities for the stories students read should be designed to engage their emotions and imaginations. Getting them to respond in this manner is called an aesthetic response (Rosenblatt, 1983; Zarillo, 1991). Aesthetic response questions and activities are designed to invite students to enter into the story, to relive it in some way, or to create associations and connections to real-life events or experiences. The prompts below reflect this aesthetic response. These can be used for class discussion, small group activities, journal entries, or as writing prompts.

Aesthetic Response Writing Prompts

1. Record a passage or part of the story that you find interesting. Tell why you recorded it.

2. Describe a time when you had a similar situation or feeling as one described in the story.

3. Which character is your favorite? Why?

4. Which character is your least favorite? Why?

5. How are you like one of the characters?

6. What do you want to write about from your reading today? What was going through your head as your read?

7. Draw an interesting book cover for this story.

8. Create a poster or advertisement that might convince others to read this story.

9. If you were a teacher, would you read this book to your class? Why?

10. What are five interesting things that happened in this story? Put them in order from happiest to saddest.

11. Ask a question of one of the characters in this story and write what you think the character's answer might be.

12. Describe a problem a character in your book faces and predict how you think that character will solve it.

13. Where and when did this story take place? Find clues to support your guess.

14. If you appeared someplace in this story, what might you see? What might you do?

15. Describe a thought or feeling that went through your head as you read.

16. What other books or movies does this story remind you of?

17. Describe something interesting or important in the story that other people might not have noticed.

18. Draw a picture, create a diagram, or design a symbol that might represent an interesting or important part of this story.

19. Describe something that might happen after the story has ended.

20. Would you recommend this book to others? What kind of person might enjoy this story?

21. Write a letter to somebody you think might like this book. Convince that person to read it.

22. Record a short dialogue in which you talk to somebody in this book.

23. Write a newspaper headline and an article for an event in this book.

24. Write a journal entry for one of the characters found in this book.

25. Break the story or chapter into beginning, middle, and ending parts. List the three most important events in each part.

26. What things in this story remind you of your life?

Evaluation/Critique

Evaluation/critique (E/C) is a postreading activity that asks students to interact with a story or book in much the same way as a movie reviewer does a movie. Some teachers call this activity *At the Library* (like *At the Movies* on TV). First, students are asked, "What are the criteria of a good book? What things make it good?" Identify and record three or four student ideas. Then tell students, "In looking at [insert story title here], how would you rate it on each criterion? How would you rate the story as a whole?"

The steps for evaluation/critique are listed below. This can be put in poster form and referred to when reteaching this skill or to guide students' thinking when they do this activity independently.

Evaluation/Critique

1. Define the criteria.

2. Look at the book/story.

3. Look at the criteria.

4. Rate the book/story on each criterion.

5. Rate book/story as a whole.

Example: A second-grade class came up with criteria for a good story in figure 15.1. They then rated the book on these criteria. E/C is best done

---

A good story has:
1. A strong character that you like.
2. Interesting story/plot. Action. Something happens.
3. Excitement and suspense.
4. A happy ending

RATING

	1. Lead Character	2. Plot	3. Exciting	4. Happy Ending	TOTAL
Wizard of Oz	4	4	5	4	18

Key: 5 = very high; 4 = high; 3 = neutral; 2 = low; 1 = very low

Conclusion: This is a pretty good story. We recommend it.

COMPARISON BY RATING

Key: 5 = very high; 4 = high; 3 = neutral; 2 = low; 1 = very low

	1. Lead Character	2. Plot	3. Exciting	4. Happy Ending	TOTAL
Wizard of Oz	4	4	5	4	18
Cinderella	4	5	5	5	19
Jack & Beanstalk	4	4	4	4	15
3 Bears	3	3	3	3	12

Conclusion: Cinderella is the best story of the four evaluated.

COMPARISON BY RANKING

Ranking: 1 = best in that category; 4 = worst in that category.

	1. Lead Character	2. Plot	3. Exciting	4. Happy Ending	TOTAL
Wizard of Oz	2	1	2	2	7
Cinderella	1	2	3	1	7
Jack & Beanstalk	3	3	1	3	10
3 Bears	4	4	4	4	15

Conclusion: Cinderella is the best story of the four evaluated.

Figure 15.1. Thinking Frame for Evaluation/Critique

in small groups as it promotes discussion and invites students to use story details to make their case.

Comparison by rating. E/C can also be used to rate and compare two or more stories. In comparison by rating each story is rated separately and the totals are used to determine which is the best (see figure 15.1).

Comparison by ranking. In comparison by ranking students rank the stories from highest to lowest in each criterion category. Totals are again used to determine which is best.

Students eventually discover that they can't rate and evaluate a fairy tale in the same way that they evaluate and rate historical fiction or an information book. This leads naturally to discussion of genre as student develop different criteria for different kinds of books.

Generic rating/review form. The generic book rating form below is an open-ended form that can be used to review a single book. When completed these should be displayed on a bulletin board or wall to create literate conversations and to entice students to read books they may not ordinarily consider.

Generic Book Rating Form
Name of Book:

Rating:

I	2	3	4	5	6	7	8	9	10
Stinker									Wow

Reason for rating:

Reviewer:

Problem Solving: CPS and MEA

Sometimes referred to as problem-based learning, this is a postreading activity using one of the two simple problem-solving strategies, creative problem solving (CPS) or means end analysis (MEA), to find a solution for a story-based or text-based problem. (This can be used with narrative or expository text.)

CPS. Creative problem solving (CPS) is a fairly simple problem-solving strategy. First, identify and define a problem found in the story or text. Students then work in pairs, small group, or large group to generate as many ideas for a solution as they can. It's important to generate a large number of ideas without evaluating them. After all possible ideas are listed, students then choose one idea that seems to be the best. (Often, two or three of the ideas will be combined for the solution.) Finally, students elaborate, refine, and share their solution. This solution could be shared in a journal, speech or oral presentation, drama, reader's theater, poster, CPS graphic organizer, picture, cartoon, journal entry, short story, picture book, or small group discussion.

CPS
1. Identify and define the problem.
2. Generate as many solution ideas as possible.
3. Choose a solution idea that seems best.
4. Elaborate and refine.
5. Share or communicate.

Problem:
Ideas:
1.
2.
3.
4.
5.
Best solution:
Refine and elaborate:

Means End Analysis

Means end analysis (MEA) is a problem-solving strategy that begins by describing the end state (see below). To help students with a possible end state, ask questions such as: "What is the goal? What outcome would I like to bring about? What would it look like if this problem were solved?" Then students analyze and describe the current state. Next, they generate a list of steps or conditions necessary to get to the desired state. You might ask questions such as: "What things need to occur? What conditions are needed to make this happen? How could this end come about? What could be done to help read the goal or end state?" The steps or conditions do not have to be in order of any kind. Finally, students construct a plan that will move them from point A (current state) to point B (desired state). The steps listed in this final plan should be in chronological order. Just like the CPS above, students can work individually, with a partner, or in groups. As well, students' final plans should be shared.

MEA
1. Describe the desired state.
2. Describe the current state.
3. Generate a list of necessary conditions or events.
4. Construction and implement a plan.
5. Share or communicate.

Goal/end state: Dorothy and the Wicked Witch become friends.
Necessary steps/things to do:
1. Dorothy needs to understand the Witch.
2. The Witch needs to become more sensitive to the needs and feelings of others.
3. The Witch won't listen until she has less power. With all her power she'll keep trying to do bad things.
4. The Witch needs to be in a position where she'll listen.
5. The Witch needs to find her sunny side and be happy.
6. The Witch needs to feel that Dorothy understands her.
7. The Witch needs to know how her actions affect Dorothy.
Current state: The Witch wants to kill Dorothy to get the magic slippers. This is not good for any friendship. Dorothy is afraid of the Witch.
The plan:

Internet Search Terms

Problem solving: *problem-based-learning-reading, problem-based-learning-literature.*

Aesthetic response: *aesthetic-response-reading, aesthetic-response-literature, aesthetic-response-activities-reading, aesthetic-response-activities-literature.*

Inferences: *making-inferences-reading, making-inferences-literature, activities-making-inferences, teaching-inference.*

References

Rosenblatt, L. M. (1983) *Literature as exploration* (fourth ed.). New York: Modern Language Association.

Zarillo, J. (1991) Theory becomes practice: Aesthetic teaching with literature. *The New Advocate, 4*, 221–34.

CHAPTER SIXTEEN
ACTIVITIES FOR EXPOSITORY TEXT

The chapter describes strategies and activities that can be used with expository text. Keep in mind, however, that many of the activities in the last two chapters can be adapted for use with expository text as well. In the same way, some of the strategies here can also be adapted for use with narrative text.

Strategies and Activities to Use with Expository Text

Reciprocal Reading

Reciprocal reading is ideal for reading textbook assignments. Here students are paired with a partner to read an assigned chapter or text. After each page or paragraph, the pair stops. One partner must cover the page and explain what they've just read to a partner as the other one looks at the page and includes missing parts. It helps with comprehension as students must attend to what they're reading and monitor comprehension. Below are the steps for a very simplified form of reciprocal reading. (I have found that most strategies work best if they're kept as simple as possible.)

Reciprocal Reading

1. Two partners read material.

2. They stop after reading a designated amount (page, paragraph, or section).

3. Partner #1 covers the page and summarizes or explains.

4. Partner #2 checks for accuracy and includes any missing material.

5. Partners read the next page, paragraph, or section.

6. Reverse roles.

Note: Works best with expository text.

I-Chart

The I-chart is a postreading activity that can be used with both expository and narrative text. After reading a story or chapter, students simply list what they consider to be the interesting or important ideas (they can list events or facts). It works best if you can identify a specific number. ("Boys and girls, try to find at least four ideas you believe are interesting or important.") Students then examine these to create a related inference or big idea. The inference or big idea may be hard for students initially, especially those who have been conditioned to believe that there can only be one right answer. The inference or big idea can be anything it makes them think about, reminds them of, or what they believe to be true. (It's impossible to get the inference or big idea wrong.)

I-Chart
Interesting or important ideas (or events or facts):

1.

2.

3.

Inference or big idea:

This activity can be done individually, but it works best with a buddy or in a small group. The I-chart could be recorded in a journal or reading log or displayed on a wall or bulletin board using a poster or large chart.

To extend this, students work individually and use the I-chart to list and examine interesting or important events that have occurred (a) in their lives, the past year, or the past week; (b) in national or local current events; (c) in the school, classroom, or community; or (d) in history during a certain period. Also, you might use the I-chart after a particular lesson as a form of review. Example: "Boys and girls, we've been looking at amphibians today in our science class. What are three interesting or important ideas that we can put on our I-chart?" After listing these ask, "Does anybody have an inference or big idea about amphibians they want to include?"

Windows

Windows is a way to see what students understand after reading expository text (or after a lesson). First, students create a window with two panes in their journal (a line down the middle of the page will work) with one side labeled "clear" and the other "fuzzy" (see figure 16.1). On the clear side they list two or three things that seem clear to them after reading the chapter. On the other side they list two to four things that are still a little fuzzy. Next, students meet in small group to see if any fuzzy things can be cleared up. Finally, the small group creates one large window to hand in. This provides you with a good sense of what you might need to reteach or review. (I use this in my college literacy methods classes as a way to determine what students understand and what I need to reteach.)

Support-A-Statement

Supporting statements with specific facts is a type of high level of thinking that proficient writers, speakers, and readers do naturally.

Clear	Fuzzy

Figure 16.1. Windows

Students at all levels can learn to do this if we make this thinking process explicit and teach it directly (Johnson, 2000). The steps are listed below:

Support-A-Statement
Use appropriate reasons, detail, or examples to support a statement, idea, or conclusion.

1. Make (or view) a statement or claim.
2. Find information/data to support the statement.
3. Organize the information (list in visual organizer).
4. Describe the original statement in terms of the new information (write a paragraph, make a speech).

As a postreading activity, the teacher first makes a statement related to some aspect of the reading. This is written on the statement blank on top of the advanced organizer (see below). Next, the students review the text that has just been read to find ideas that support that statement. These supporting ideas are then listed under the original statement. This support-a-statement is a great pairs or small group activity as it gets students talking about the text. Support-a-statement advanced organizers can be made into posters or other types of artworks (for example, the support-a-statement below could be drawn on the side of a rocket or space suit), or simply written in a journal or learning log.

Support-A-Statement
Statement: Going to Mars is dangerous.
Supporting Ideas
1. Radiation from the sun could kill you.
2. By yourself. No humans can help you.
3. Takes a long time. Need food, oxygen, and water.
4. Entering Martian atmosphere very difficult.
5. Hard to carry enough fuel.

To extend the idea, have students write a paragraph (or two) using two ideas from the support-a-statement. Note: They do not have to use all the ideas in their paragraph, just the ones that make the most sense.

Going to Mars is dangerous. First of all, it will take about two years. During this time, you're by yourself. Nobody can help you. Also, you have to take all your food, water, and air with you. If you run out, that's it. You're done. Also, you have to carry a lot of rocket fuel to get there and back.

Small Group Speeches

Small group speeches (SGS) provide students who may have difficulties reading and writing another way to demonstrate their learning. At the same time, it is open-ended and can provide choice, challenge, and complexity for highly creative or intellectually gifted students. It can be used effectively as a postreading activity for both narrative and expository text, although it seems to work best for expository text. The steps are as follows:

1. **Create a brainstorming web for a speaking topic related to the text.** (see figure 16.2). To do this, identify a topic and print it in a circle in the center of a blank sheet of paper.

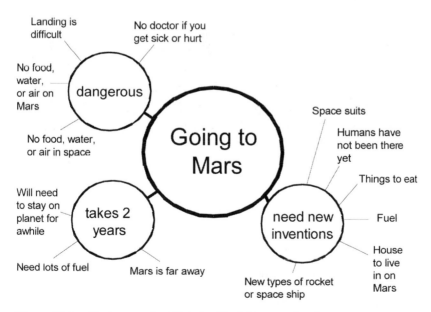

Figure 16.2.   Brainstorming Web for Oral Communication

2. **Identify two or three nodes or subtopics related to the topic.**

3. **Brainstorm to find interesting or important things about node.** Students should use only single words or short phrases to hold each idea. You will need to model this process initially by thinking aloud and drawing on a blackboard, poster, or overhead to create a brainstorming web.

4. **Use the brainstorming web as a guide to give a short speech about the topic.** This works best if students who are speaking stand up and either hold the web or set it on the desk in front of them as they speak. (You will need to model these speeches.) SGS should be no more than one minute in length for middle-grade students and thirty to forty-five seconds for primary students. (This is much longer than most students think.) Groups of three to five students should be used here. The speaker should stand as his or her speech is delivered. One student in the group should be designated as the timekeeper and calls "time" when the allotted time is up.

Using SGS, several students are able to speak in small group at the same time instead of one student speaking to the whole class. This is a much less intimidating way of developing oral communication skills. It also enables you to see many students give postreading speeches within a relatively short time span.

To extend this activity, introduce elements of oral communication (EOC; see below). Introduce no more than one or two elements at a time. Keep things relatively simple and informal during the first few weeks of using this strategy. You can eventually provide more specific feedback. Feedback is different from criticism. Feedback should always be positive, first pointing out what students did well and then identifying one or two things that they could do to improve their oral communication skills.

Elements of Oral Communication (EOC)

1. Look at your audience.

2. Use an average pace. Not too fast and not too slow.

3. Use inflection. Don't use just a monotone. Make your voice rise and fall to make listening more interesting.

4. Control your stance. Don't lean or slouch.

5. Use your hands to emphasis points.

6. Use correct grammar.

7. Use known words. Avoids slang or profanity.

8. Use words carefully. Avoids nonwords and nonphrases such as: "um," "well," "you know," and "you guys." Do not use extra words if it can be helped.

9. Be concise and to the point. Do not ramble.

The checklist for oral communication below can be used for feedback and documentation. You can also create your own checklist using EOC. It's fairly easy to sit in the middle of a class and provide feedback to two or three students as they are speaking simultaneously. When speakers seem to have developed trust within the group, you can teach students how to give feedback to each other or to themselves.

Checklist for Oral Communication
Student: _____ Grade: _____ Date: _____

Key: ✓ = trait was present
✓ + = trait was present to a greater extent
✓ − = trait was present to a lesser extent
= oops

____ speech is organized, makes sense
____ speaks in a loud voice
____ looks at the audience
____ stands on both feet
____ speaks at a comfortable pace (not too fast or too slow)

Student Comments:

Teacher Comments:

KWL Chart

This is a pre- and a postreading activity that can be done individually, in small groups, or with a whole class. To introduce the activity, put a KWL (Know, Want, Learn) chart on the blackboard or overhead. Before reading the chapter or text, ask students to list what they know about a subject in the first column and what they want to know in the second column. (This serves to activate students' prior knowledge and set the purpose for reading.) After reading ask students to make any necessary corrections in the first column and then list what they have learned in the third column.

KWL Chart

K—What do you **K**now?	**W**—What do you **W**ant to know?	**L**—What did you **L**earn?
I.	I.	I.
2.	2.	2.
3.	3.	3.

Group Read

Group read is a cooperative learning activity that enables low ability readers to interact with concepts from assigned chapters or text. It can be used to keep low ability readers from falling behind conceptually in a mixed ability classroom.

1. **Put students in mixed ability groups of three to six students.** Younger students need smaller groups (three), older students can handle larger groups (four or five). Groups should be created by the teacher and listed on the board. (Never put students in the socially awkward position of finding students for their group.) Strive to have balance in terms of high ability and low ability readers in each group. A word of caution: Do not put your high ability readers in the role of tutor. This is unfair to them.

2. **Assign roles.** Each student should have a chance to be the leader or the president. The president makes all final decisions and, most important, assigns the roles. To determine the pres-

ident, use some sort of question in which students must talk with each other to find the answer. For example: "Who in your group last ate vegetables? Who last sang a song? Who is the youngest? This person is the president today." This gets students talking with each other, which serves to improve trust among the group.

Ideally, you'd like students who are comfortable reading out loud to be the readers. Two ideas you might try: First, you could identify the readers in each group ahead of time. Simply put a check mark next to their name as you write the groups on the board. Second, allow the president to make the selection with the rule that readers can tag team (like in professional wrestling) or pass to another when they get tired. Below are some of the other roles you might consider for group read.

Roles for Group Read

President: makes all final decisions, assigns roles.

Reader/s: one or two people who read the text out loud.

Note taker/s: one or two people who record the important ideas.

Idea pointer: points out the important ideas.

Artist: demonstrates one or more of the important ideas visually using a diagram or pictures.

Speaker: presents ideas to the rest of the class.

Mime: makes a nonverbal display to illustrate the ideas the speaker is presenting.

3. **Students read.** Everyone should have a copy of the text to be read so they can read along. Idea pointers point out important ideas as the text is being read. To do this, allow one or two students to make a pencil dot next to the sentence in the book that has an important idea. In this way, the flow of the reading is not interrupted.

4. **Idea pointers point and note takers note.** At the end of the chapter or article, idea pointers refer back to their pencil dots in order to share what they thought to be interesting or important ideas. The group then decides if they want the note

taker to record it. Ideally, there are two note takers so that as one idea is being recorded you can discuss the next one.

5. **Students engage in some postreading product or perform-ance.** At the end of group read students must create some product or performance that relies on them having read the chapter or text. This product or performance should be such that you could point to it and answer yes or no as to whether students were successful. What particular products or per-formance might you use? Pick any that have been described in this text.

Internet Search Terms

Postreading activities: *reciprocal-reading, KWL, activities-expository-reading, cooperative-learning-reading, expository-text-graphic-organizer.*

References

Johnson, A. (2000) *Up and out: Using creative and critical thinking to enhance learning.* Boston: Allyn and Bacon.

SHARED READING AND GUIDED READING

Although they share similar elements, shared reading and guided reading are technically two different strategies used for different purposes (see figure 17.1). Shared reading is done with a large group of students of varying reading ability levels. The purpose here is to interact with the ideas found in the text or story. Guided reading is done with a small group of students of similar reading levels, students who have a similar skill deficit, or with one student. The purpose here is to work on specific reading strategies or skills. Both are valuable tools that can be used to enhance literacy instruction; however, like any tool, they should not be used all the time. Put another way, reading or guided reading should not be the sole means of reading instruction.

Shared Reading

Shared reading enables the whole class to share insights or enter into a common discussion around a book or text. Here students of all ability levels interact with new concepts, see new vocabulary words in authentic contexts, and engage in high level thinking and creative activities. (Note: Having a reading disability does not mean that students have a thinking disability. Students at all reading levels need to have opportunities to engage in these types of activities.) In shared reading, students read along with the teacher; however, *it is not round robin reading*. (Round robin reading is where you go around the class and each student is asked to read a paragraph.)

Shared Reading – Interact with Ideas	Similarities ↓	Guided Reading – Teach and Reinforce Skills
1. Whole class reads the same text.	1. Students share the same story or text.	1. A small flexible groups read the same text.
2. The goal is to interact with ideas; however, it can involve work on word identification, comprehension, and thinking strategies	2. Can be done with narrative or expository text. 3. With younger students, use big books or picture books. 4. With older students, use (a) textbooks, (b) photocopied articles, (c) articles or text passages on an overhead, (d) articles or text passages on power point, or (e) articles or text passages on a computer or website.	2. The goal is to work on word identification, comprehension, and thinking strategies; however, it can involve interacting with ideas.
3. *Can* involve some amount of silent reading.		3. *Should* involve silent reading or whisper reading.
4. Interact with ideas first; teach skills second.		4. Teach skills first, interact with ideas second.
5. Reading material is at or beyond students' instruction reading level.	5. Social interaction is important (one a whole class, small group, or pairs) 6. Not the sole means of reading instruction.	5. Reading material is at students' instructional level.

↑ differences   ↑ differences

Figure 17.1. Compare-O-Graph: Shared Reading and Guided Reading

Primary grades. In the primary grades shared reading is usually done using a picture book or a big book with students sitting together on a carpet in the front of the room. Here you read while students simply listen. With big books use choral reading, echo reading, or have students read along silently as you point to individual words.

Intermediate grades and above. In the intermediate grades and above, shared reading is usually done with a novel, textbook, magazine article, newspaper article, or even a website. (And yes, shared reading is a strategy that is appropriate for middle school and high school.) Text can be photocopied, put on an overhead projector, or displayed using PowerPoint. The important thing is that all students need to be able to see and read the text. Students then follow along as the teacher reads or they read the text silently to themselves (see ERT below). Choral and echo reading should not be used at this level.

Everybody-read-to (ERT). Reading a large amount of text may be overwhelming for some students in a mixed ability shared reading experience. This silent reading strategy can be used with intermediate grades and above to alleviate this. Students are told to read to a particular point, usually one to four paragraphs at a time depending on the level. Examples:

- *"Everybody read to the second paragraph on page 23. I'll be asking you to identify one interesting or important idea. Look up when you have finished."*

- *"Billy seems to be angry. I wonder what will happen next. Read to the bottom of page 7 to find out. Raise your thumb when you finish so that I know."*

Students read silently to that spot and wait for your question or activity. Slower readers are usually able to get enough of the information to participate in the discussion. What they don't read, however, they're able to assimilate through the discussion that takes place.

Planning a Shared Reading Experience

The steps for planning a shared reading experience are as follows:

1. **Select and preview text to be read.** Initially, the piece of text chosen should be relatively short. As you and your students become more comfortable with this process, longer texts can be used. For older students, look for text that's related to a unit being studied or a book currently being read in a literature class.

2. **Decide on the type of reading material.** Decide whether you will read a big book, picture book, photocopied text, text on overhead, text on PowerPoint, or website.

3. **Decide on the mode of reading.** Listen silently, ERT, or a combination. For younger students there may be times to use choral reading or echo reading.

4. **Design a prereading activity.** Use any of the prereading strategies described in this book to provide an overview and to engage students' interest.

5. **Create structure and design questions and activities.** Look for appropriate places within the text to stop (use ERT for older students). Design text-related questions or activities for

use here. Students eventually learn to ask these kinds of questions themselves as they are reading.

6. **Design a postreading activity.** Use any of the postreading activities described in this text to get students to interact with the text and with each other.

Questions for Shared Reading: Narrative Text

These questions are designed for shared reading experiences with narrative text.

To preview:
- What do you think this story is about? What clues do you see in the title or cover of the book?
- What does the title tell us?
- What are some interesting things you see on the cover of the book?
- What do you know about _____?

To check for understanding:
- What is the story about?
- What is the problem?
- What do I want to know more about?
- What do I know about . . . ?
- What doesn't make sense to you?

To associate:
- What are you thinking about right now? Why?
- What does this story remind you of? Are there events that are similar to another story or to events in your life (compare-o-graph)?
- Who does this character remind you of? Is this character similar to another character you know in another story or in real life (compare-o-graph)?

To notice:
- What is an interesting description that you noticed?
- What new or interesting word did you notice?
- What important story clue did you notice?

To elaborate:
- How might you make that sentence more interesting?
- What kind of character would you add to the story?

To predict-verify-decide:
- What's going to happen next?
- What are some important clues? (Use the predict-o-graph)
- How do you think this story will end?

To infer:
- What does this tell us about that character?
- Based on story clues, what happened before/next?
- How does _____ feel about _____?

To imagine or visualize:
- What do you image this (person, place, or thing) looks like?
- What does this scene look like to you? What are some things you would see if you were there? What picture is painted in your mind?

To summarize:
- What are the important events that have happened so far?
- What's happened so far? Who did what?

To decide:
- What do you think _____ should do?
- How might _____ solve this problem?
- What would you do if you were _____?

* Use any of the aesthetic response questions described in chapter 16.
** Use any of the activities described in chapters 15 and 16.

Questions for Shared Reading: Expository Text

These questions are designed for shared reading experiences with expository text.

To preview:
- What do you think this chapter/article is about? What clues do you see in the title or cover of the book?

- What does the title tell us?
- What are some interesting things you see on the cover of the book?

To check for understanding:
- What is this chapter about?
- What are three important ideas?
- What do you want to know more about?
- What do I know about . . . ?
- Should we reread the paragraph?

To elaborate and connect:
- How might you restate that sentence?
- How could it be stated more clearly?
- How might you make that sentence more interesting?

Questions for during reading:
- What things are a little fuzzy?
- How else do you think _____ could be applied?
- How could _____ be changed, modified, or elaborated?
- What are the main parts of _____?
- How would you compare this to _____?
- What's the main idea in this paragraph?

To summarize:
- What are the important ideas so far?
- What do you hope to learn more about?
- How would you explain _____?
- How would you define _____?

* Also, use any of the activities described in chapter 17.

Guided Reading

Although there are differing interpretations of guided reading, most would agree that it's a strategy used to help individuals or small groups of students work on a particular skill or skills. These skills include word identification, comprehension, and thinking strategies.

Planning a Guided Reading Experience

The steps are as follows:

1. **Identify students and instructional needs.** The groups used for guided reading are formed based on a skill deficit the teacher has observed during reading conferences or at other times. Thus, the students in each group vary from session to session based on need. Guided reading groups are small and flexible, and comprise one to eight students (although smaller is better). Keep the sessions focused and purposeful by identifying a specific skill or skills to learn or practice. (Don't try to teach too many skills in one guided reading session.)

2. **Identify suitable text at approximate instructional level.** The text used should be as close to students' instructional reading levels as possible. This means they can read approximately 90 percent of the words.

3. **Decide on the type of reading material.** Liked shared reading above, you could use big book, picture book, photocopied text, text on overhead, text on PowerPoint, or text found on a website (if everyone has access to a computer). However, most often students have a physical copy of the text in front of them (an actual book or photocopy of a book or article).

4. **Design prereading activities.** Prereading activities are designed to get students ready to read the upcoming selection. The goal is to model and teach the types of strategies that efficient readers use before they read. Below are prereading activities that can be used for expository text and narrative text.

Prereading Activities for Expository Text
Paragraphs
- Read the first and last paragraph.
- Students identify what they know about the topic.

Title and Headings
- Examine the title and heading.
- Students identify what they know about the topic.
- Students whisper read or read silently.

Outline
- Create an outline of chapter content.
- Review.
- Students identify what they know about the topic.
- Students whisper read or read silently.

Preteach
- Preteach important concepts that students will read.
- Students whisper read or read silently.

KWL
- Students list what they know (K) about topic.
- Students list what they want (W) to know about topic.
- Students whisper read or read silently.
- After reading, students list what they have learned (L).
- Students make necessary connections to what they know (K).

Activate Background Knowledge
- Students identify what they know about the topic.
- Ideas are listed on the board.
- Students whisper read or read silently.

Connect Two
- Follow the instructions listed in chapter 12.
- Students whisper read or read silently

Graphic Organizer or Semantic Map
- Follow the instructions listed in chapter 12.
- Students whisper read or read silently.

Prereading Activities for Narrative Text
Preview/Overview
- Provide a general overview of the story (like a movie preview).
- Set the hook ("Read to find out what happens when . . .").
- Students whisper read or read silently.

Outline
- Create an outline of story events.
- Review.
- Students make predictions.
- Students whisper read or read silently.

Story Map
- Create a story map of important events.
- Review.
- Students whisper read or read silently.

- **Introduce Characters**
- Identify important characters.
- Provide brief description.
- Students whisper read or read silently.

Story Grammar
- Identify important characters.
- Identify problem or issue.
- Identify setting.
- Set the hook ("Read to find out how they solve this problem").
- Students whisper read or read silently.

Connect Two
- Follow the instructions listed in chapter 12.
- Students whisper read or read silently.

Predicting
- Provide general overview.
- Teacher reads to important event.
- Ask students to predict what will happen next.
- Students whisper read or read silently.

5. **Create structure and design instruction.** Look for appropriate places within the text to stop for instruction and modeling of specific skills. Instruction should be designed to teach word identification skills, comprehension skills, or thinking strategies (shown below). Focus on one to three skills or strategies in each guided reading session. In your instruction, use instances of teacher think-aloud to model your thinking.

<u>Word Identification Skills</u>
- Context clues. Figuring out what the word is by looking at what makes sense in the sentence.
- PSR/morphemic analysis. Figuring out what the word is by looking at the prefix, suffix, or root word.

- Word analysis. Figuring out what the word is by looking at word families or parts of the word you recognize.
- Ask a friend. Turn to a friend and say, "What's this word?"
- Skip the word. If you are still creating meaning, why stop the process to figure out a word?
- Phonics. Using minimal letter cues in combination with context clues to figure out what the word is.

(See chapter 4)

Comprehension Skills

Prereading Comprehension Skills
- Preview/Overview
- Web and Brainstorm
- Outline and Brainstorm

During-Reading Comprehension Skills
- Paragraph Reread
- Read and Pause

Postreading Comprehension Skills
- Article Reread
- Webbing and Outlining

(See chapter 13)

Thinking Strategies
- Predicting (predict-o-graph)
- Inferring (infer-o-graph, character map, person chart, head chart)
- Comparing (compare-o-graph, comparing T-chart, comparison chart, attribute chart)
- Summarizing (story maps, story grammar)
- Analyzing (story analysis, plot profile, orderizer)
- Determining cause-effect relationships (cause-effect-o-graph)
- Finding supporting ideas (support-a-statement, web)
- Making connections or associations (double journal entry, head connector, adjective fun, CPS, MEA)
- Evaluating (evaluation/critique)

(See chapters 14, 15, and 16.)

This is an example of how you might use teacher think-aloud to teach word analysis:

The teacher reads the following sentence from the text: "The piano player developed automaticity so that he could perform the skill without thinking."

The teacher uses think-aloud to teach a word identification strategy: (*Points to the word, "automaticity."*) "Hmmm, I'm not quite sure about that word. I do see parts of it that I know. 'Auto' or 'automatic.' That means that something does it by itself. I also see 'city.' I think it's pronounced auto-ma-tic-ity. It must be related to automatic somehow. The sentence tells me that it means doing something without thinking about it. Let me reread the sentence to see if that makes sense."

6. **Decide on the mode of reading.** Usually, students will read the text in one of three ways: (a) follow along silently as the teacher reads aloud, (b) read the text silently to themselves (use ERT), or (c) whisper read (this allows you to listen in). There may be times with younger students when it is appropriate to use the following: (a) buddy reading (students pair up with a partner and read sections out loud to each other), (b) choral reading, and (c) echo reading. Choral and echo reading can be used to develop reading fluency. As always, adopt and adapt to meet your needs.

7. **Design a postreading activity.** Use any of the postreading activities described in this text to get students to interact with the text and with each other.

Internet Search Terms

Shared reading: *shared-reading, shared-reading-activities, shared-reading-methods, shared-reading-lesson-plans, shared-reading-instruction, shared-reading-graphic-organizers.*

Guided reading: *guided-reading, guided-reading-activities, guided-reading-methods, guided-reading-lesson-plans, guided-reading-instruction, guided-reading-graphic-organizers.*

PART THREE
INFORMATION AND STRATEGIES FOR TUTORING AND TEACHING WRITING

THE PROCESS OF WRITING

W e learned in chapter 2 that all language processes are connected (reading, writing, speaking, listening, and thinking). Each language process enhances students' ability to use the others. Thus, one way to help children become more fluent in their reading is to help them become more fluent writers. This chapter describes the five-step writing process and strategies for generating ideas for writing topics.

The Five-Step Writing Process

The five-step process writing approach described by Donald Graves (1983) is presented here. This will provide a context for the writing activities found in the next chapters.

Step 1: Prewriting.   The goal here is to generate ideas. Listing, brainstorming, outlining, silent thinking, conversation with a neighbor, or power writing (described below) are all ways to generate ideas.

Step 2: Drafting.   Drafting is the writer's first attempt to capture ideas on paper. Quantity here is valued over quality. If done correctly, the draft is a rambling, disconnected accumulation of ideas. Most of the writing activities in the classroom involve just these first two steps. Only those drafts that students feel are interesting or of value should be taken to the next step (Donald Graves calls these hot topics).

Step 3: Revising.   This is the heart of the writing process. Here a piece is revised and reshaped many times. The draft stage is like throwing a large blob of clay on the potter's wheel. Revising is where you shape the blob, adding parts, taking parts away, adding parts, and continually molding and changing. Here you look for flow and structure. You reread paragraphs and move things around.

Again, not every draft should be taken to this stage. Graves recommends that students be given a choice as to which of these drafts they want to take to the revision step. Generally, students find only one in five drafts worthy of investing the mental and emotional energy necessary to revise and create a finished product. The rest of the story drafts can be kept in a file folder as a junkyard for other writing ideas or included in a portfolio to document students' writing journeys.

Step 4: Editing. This is the stage where grammar, spelling, and punctuation errors are corrected. A word of caution: The quickest way to ruin a good writing project or damage a writer is to insist that step 4 be included in step 1, 2, or 3. If writers are editing or worrying about mechanics at the prewriting, drafting, and revising stages, the flow of ideas and the quality of writing suffers. Precious brain space that is devoted to generating and connecting ideas will instead be utilized worrying about writing mechanics.

One last thing about the editing phase: Real writers (of which I am one) edit their writing at the end. Real writers also rely on editors, spell check, and grammar check. In teaching your students to become authors and composers of authentic writing, teach them to approximate the writing process used by real writers. That is, set up peer editing groups and teach students how to use the grammar and spelling functions on a word processor.

Step 5: Publishing and sharing. This is where students' writing is shared with an audience. Writing becomes real and alive at this point. Publishing can involve putting together class books, collections of writing, school or class newspapers, school or class magazines, or displaying short samples of writing in the hall or out in the community. Writing experiences become even more powerful by having students read their work out loud in small groups, to another classmate, or in a large group setting (see chapter 19 for publishing ideas).

Strategies for Getting Writing Ideas

To the greatest extent possible, you should provide opportunities for students to select writing topics that they care about, topics that invite them to say what it is they want to say. This will create greater motivation to write, which, in turn, will improve students' writing and communicating skills and result in a more interesting and engaged classroom or tutoring session. However, if students aren't used to selecting their writing topics they may need a little help. Four strategies for getting writing ideas are described here.

Teacher writing prompts.   Sometimes it is appropriate for the teacher to provide a writing prompt or unfinished sentence (see chapter 20 for writing prompts). The trick in designing good teacher-direct writing prompts is to make them specific, universal, and open-ended.

An example of a poor writing prompt would be "Describe a favorite family vacation." This is a poor writing prompt because you cannot assume that every student (a) has a family, (b) feels comfortable with his or her family, (c) has had a family vacation, (d) wants to go on a vacation, or (e) enjoys family vacations. With this writing prompt you are telling students, "You must have a family you enjoy and you must have enjoyed a vacation someplace. If not, you are abnormal."

Instead, an example of a good writing prompt would be something like "Describe something you enjoy doing." Every student, regardless of circumstance, could respond to this prompt. Every student could succeed regardless of ability.

Brain walk.   This technique should be demonstrated to students in large group a few times. Here you simply take your brain out for a walk. First, write a word at the top of a sheet of thinking paper (scratch paper) or a journal page. Then identify the first thought or idea that pops into your head. Use a word or short phrase to capture it. Don't write complete sentences here. Instead, use a word or the fewest words possible to hold the idea. Here are the steps for a brain walk:

1. Write word on top of paper.

2. Identify first thought or image.

3. Use word or phrase to capture it.

4. Move to next thought or image.

5. Repeat until the page is full.

If done correctly, the brain walk shouldn't make sense to anybody except the writer. (See my brain walk below.) A good brain walk will usually provide three or four good ideas to use for stories. Students should record these story ideas in their writing journals or writing portfolios. They can then refer back to this topic list whenever they're looking for writing ideas.

My brain walk: balloon - circus - circus in Grantsburg - fairgrounds - fairs - burning down the animal barn - carnival games - playing games in junior high - squeaky voices - mice - Stuart Little - fifth-grade class - football - recess - Sam - working hard - state fair - rides - sick - away from work - resting - sleeping - big fluffy bed - staying at Grandma's house - rice pudding - thick oatmeal - eating breakfast with grandpa - paper route - cold winter - snowmobiling - frozen fingers - chopper mittens

List of things. Here students designate a page in a writing journal or portfolio where they keep lists of things. These things have the potential to produce stories. Students should be encouraged to add to their list as they think of new things or new writing ideas. As you can see in the thing chart below, I use categories to help students think of things.

Thing Chart

Things I Notice	Happy Things	New Things
1.	1.	1.
2.	2.	2.
3.	3.	3.

Events	Important Things	Old Things
1.	1.	1.
2.	2.	2.
3.	3.	3.

The steps for creating a list of things are as follows:

1. Designate a page in your journal or writing log.

2. List ideas that sound interesting.

3. List things you notice.

4. List interesting or important events.

5. List things that make you sad, happy, angry, or bored.

Noticing tours. Noticing tours can be done two ways. First, actually go outside and notice things. Look for sights, sounds, smells, textures, and feelings. Have students take their writing logs with them. Direct them to notice things for each sense: "What do you hear? Write it down. What does it remind you of? What do you see? What's interesting about it? What does it make you think about?"

The second way to do a noticing tour is through imagery. Start with something simple like "Think back to your trip to school today. What did you notice?" Then, just like above, take the students through each of the senses. Or you could ask students to think of a favorite place, an interesting place they've visited, or a place they'd like to visit.

Looking Ahead

The next chapters provide specific strategies and activities for each stage of the five-step writing process.

Internet Search Terms

The process of writing: *process-writing, 5-step-writing process, five-step-writing-process, writing-process-activities, generating-ideas-writing, writing-ideas.*

References

Graves, D. (1983) *Writing: Teachers and children at work.* Portsmouth, N.H.: Heinemann.

STRATEGIES FOR PREWRITING, DRAFTING, REVISING, EDITING, AND PUBLISHING

This chapter describes and demonstrates a variety of strategies and activities for each phase of the five-step writing process.

Prewriting Strategies for Generating Ideas for Writing

What writers do before writing is just as important as what happens during the writing process. Below are described seven prewriting strategies that can be used to generate ideas before students begin writing their drafts.

Power write.   Here students write continuously for one to three minutes (a shorter duration for younger students, longer for older students). This is different from the free write where students generally write at a slower pace for five to ten minutes. This is also different from the brain walk described in the last chapter because here students are writing complete sentences. The power write is designed to get students to write quickly without thinking. Evaluating gets in the way of idea generation and should be avoided. Here you want students to associate (quickly make connections) but think very little.

To do this, students start with a writing topic (or any word idea) and quickly associate. They should keep their pencil moving, recording sentences and ideas, freely hopping from one idea to the next. The key is to catch and record the very first thought or image that comes to mind. If done correctly, the writing should be a jumbled and disjointed mess. You will need to demonstrate how to do this by thinking out loud as you record your ideas. The steps for power write are described below. These should be written out in poster form to use as a teaching guide and reminder.

Power Write

1. Find an idea.

2. Associate: attach first word or image that comes to mind.

3. Write quickly: keep the pencil moving.

4. Write for two to three minutes.

5. Look for ideas to use. Begin draft.

Below is an example of my power write. I started with the word "dog" and wrote the first thing that came to mind. I wasn't concerned with order or a logical flow of ideas. I wanted to simple create a pile of gravel out of which I might find a couple of precious nuggets for writing topics. After doing my power write I discovered three interesting ideas that I can make into stories.

My power write: Dog. Ran out into the street. My dog Mickey likes to run. Got to be very careful. Have a leash on when you open the door. Don't want him run over. A friendly dog. Emotionally needy. Snuggles on my pillow in bed. Do we spoil our dog? Seems to have his own mind. He reflects parts of me. Dog owners. Projecting. Cesar Millan. TV show. The Dog Whisperer, tries to help people understand their dogs. Understanding people and situations is the key. People are not irrational beings. People are sometimes nonrational. People are rational with bad rationale. People are rational with poor motives. Selfishness, self-centeredness, ego sometimes overpowers our ability to reason. We make decisions using knowledge, reason, our emotions, and our intuitions. Using too much of any one leaves us out of balance. We then make bad decisions. Do we project?

Brainstorm and group.   With this prewriting skill you start with a writing topic, then simply list as many related things as you can. This is different from the power write in that you simply list a series of words to hold the idea. In power writing you record the idea and write sentences or parts of sentences. As stated in an earlier chapter, when brainstorming ideas, they should be listed without evaluation. Crazy unrelated ideas are just as important as those that seem more pragmatic as they all help you see things differently. Once all ideas are listed, then you can start looking for groups or patterns to emerge. Put similar ideas together to create groups. The steps are listed here:

Brainstorm and Group

1. Start with a topic.

2. Generate as many ideas as you can.

3. Look for groups or patterns.

4. Organize into groups.

5. Use groups for sections or paragraphs.

Again, you will need to demonstrate how to brainstorm and group by doing one together (thinking out loud as you do it). Do this using the brainstorm and group chart below. In this case I started with my writing topic (my dog Mickey). Then I listed (a) things I know about dogs, pugs, and Mickey, (b) things related to Mickey, and (c) things I might want to say about Mickey. These ideas were recorded in list form on the left side of the brainstorm and group chart below. (If I were demonstrating to a small group or whole class, I would use an overhead projector, a large poster, or the front board.) Then, thinking out loud (cognitive modeling), I began to look for similar ideas to use in creating groups. I initially found three categories. I then started listing ideas under each category in the column on the right. All ideas were eventually put in a group. I found that putting the initial ideas into groups helped me generate additional ideas for each category. (This process of creating groups and organizing ideas into groups leads naturally to talking about structure and paragraphs.) The end result of this was a three-part structure that I used to write a draft about my dog, Mickey.

Brainstorm and Group Chart

IDEAS

<u>My Dog Mickey</u>

My dog Mickey

Pugs

Friendly

Wags his butt

Mind of his own

Sheds

Loves to eat

Cries if left alone

Small dog

Lots of energy

Two years old

Got him at nine weeks

Chose him from a group of four dogs

First saw him at three weeks—looked like a rat

Pug traits: friendly, easygoing, likes to play

IDEAS PUT INTO GROUPS

<u>Pug Traits</u>

Friendly

Pug traits: friendly, easygoing, likes to play

Shed

Short hair

Snout

Snore

<u>Getting Mickey</u>

My dog Mickey

First saw him at three weeks—looked like a rat

Got him at nine weeks

Chose him from a group of four dogs

Took him home

He cried at night

<u>My Dog Mickey</u>

Friendly

Wags his butt

Loves to eat

Loves to be with people
Two years old

Outlining.   Start with the writing topic, then look for two to four main ideas related to the topic. Most writers discover that finding supporting details for each of the main ideas becomes much easier once the flexible outline has been written. Allow new ideas to appear or old ideas to melt away, merge, or appear in other places as you are working through the draft and revision stages. The steps for outlining are listed here:

Outlining

1. Look at topic or theme.

2. List important ideas using numbers.

3. Use letters to add details.

4. Begin writing

Here is an example of the outline I used to write a story about my dog, Mickey:

Mickey the Dog
I. Traits
   1. Happy
   2. Friendly
   3. Likes to snuggle
   4. Needs attention
II. Care
   1. Sheds
   2. Watch what he eats
      a. Can get overweight
      b. Feed three-quarter cup of food twice a day
   3. Brush often
   4. Walks
      a. Every day
      b. Tire him out
      c. Keep him slim and healthy
   5. Housebreaking
      a. Six months
      b. Did everything wrong

III. My Dog Mickey
    1. Deciding on a pug
       a. Saw a friend's
       b. Loved the friendliness of it
    2. Saw a pug when I was out running
    3. Adopting and selecting Mickey
    4. The early days

Web and brainstorm. Web and brainstorm provides the same type of structure as an outline; however, the process is more spatial and more visually stimulating for some students. Here you start with a writing topic as a central bubble, then look for two to four related ideas for nodes (see figure 19.1). With younger students it's recommended that only two nodes be used. The steps are listed here:

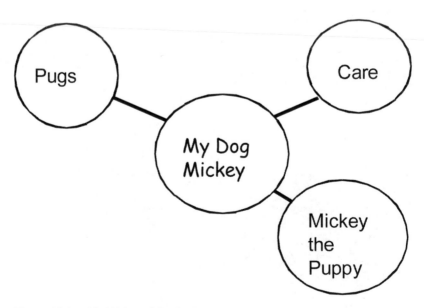

Figure 19.1. My Web and Brainstorm

Web and Brainstorm

1. Find a writing topic (central bubble).

2. Identify two to four subideas (nodes).

3. Brainstorm on each node.

4. Each node becomes a paragraph.

5. Begin writing draft.

Brainstorm. The goal in brainstorming is quantity of ideas. Students do not naturally know how to brainstorm; thus, you must teach and demonstrate the process. If everyone is writing on a similar topic, brainstorming can be an effective prewriting activity to do in large group. As students see the ideas of others they get more ideas for their own writing projects. For example, let's say we were writing about things that annoy us. I would say, "Boys and girls, I know I really get annoyed when somebody butts into line. What are some things that annoy you?" As students volunteer ideas, they would be recorded on the board. The specific steps for brainstorming are listed here:

Brainstorm

1. Look at the idea.

2. List as many ideas as quickly as you can.

3. Begin writing

There are four rules for brainstorming listed below. Put these rules in poster form to assist your initial brainstorming instruction, and then use this poster for quick review when needed.

Rules for Brainstorming

1. *All ideas must be accepted.* No criticizing or evaluation is allowed. At this stage, bad ideas are just as important as good ideas.

2. *Freewheeling is celebrated.* Creative, bizarre, unusual, and silly ideas are welcomed along with smart-aleck comments and

random associations. All of these can be used to stretch our thinking and get us thinking more broadly.

3. *The goal of brainstorming is quantity.* The more ideas we have, the greater our choice is in finding a solution.

4. *Hitchhiking is welcome.* Hitchhiking is when you add to an idea that has already been stated or combine two or more ideas. This is a technique many creative problem solvers use.

Turn to a neighbor. Things don't have to be complicated to be effective. Explaining our initial ideas or listening to the ideas of others is a simple, effective prewriting strategy. For example, I might say, "Today we're writing about things we noticed on the way to school. Take a minute, turn to a neighbor. Share at least two things you noticed on the way to school." These are the steps:

Turn to a Neighbor

1. Find a topic or theme.

2. Turn to a neighbor and share.

3. Listen, ask questions, add ideas.

4. Begin writing.

List four. The last prewriting strategy is listing. Here students start with an idea or writing topic. They must quickly list four words or ideas associated with their writing topic on top of their page before writing. These are the steps:

List Four

1. Start with an idea.

2. Quickly list four words that come to your mind.

3. Begin writing.

The Draft—Sloppy Copy

As stated in the last chapter, the draft (sometimes called a sloppy copy) is where students make the first attempt to capture their ideas on paper. Again, most of the writing activities you do in class will involve just the prewrite and draft stages. Drafts are put in students' individual portfolios (a manila file folder kept in a box or milk carton someplace). Students can then choose which draft they want to bring into the revision stage.

Getting responses to story drafts makes them become more alive and provides ideas for the revision stage. However, responses do not (should not) always have to come from a teacher or parent. Students' responding to each other's stories often creates a more powerful writing experience. Below are four simple ideas for responding to drafts:

Partner oral response. Here students turn to a neighbor and read their story draft out loud. They could also simply describe some of the main ideas. The partner then responds orally to the ideas. You will, however, have to teach students how to respond to each other's writing in a positive, supportive manner. The response guidelines listed below can be used here. Put these on a poster to use as a reference (you may wish to include others). Tell students that these are just hints if they don't know what to say.

Oral Response Guidelines

1. What did you like?

2. What did you want to know more about?

3. What might be added to make it more interesting?

4. What did it remind you of?

Small group oral response. In small groups, students read or describe a journal entry. These entries become natural vehicles for small group discussions as members of the group respond.

Trade and respond. Students trade writing drafts with a partner and write their responses right on the page. You can also use groups of three or more students, having them write and rotate stories until everybody has responded to each. In this way the draft becomes a living entity with a collection of perspectives.

Whole class response. At the end of every writing session choose one or two volunteers to read their story drafts to the class or tutoring group. This differs slight from the author's chair (described below) where students read their edited pieces to the class.

Revising, Editing, and Publishing

This section provides ideas for revising, editing, and publishing.

Revising

Donald Graves (1983) says that generally only one out of five drafts are hot—meaning that they are worthy of being taken to the revision stage. Once a student has taken a piece to the revision stage, the majority of time should be spent reading, rereading, moving things around, and getting feedback from others. This is where time is spent molding and shaping a piece of writing. Encourage students to read their work out loud to develop a writer's ear.

Magic circle. The goal of feedback and response is to see how the writing is playing in the heads of the readers. One strategy you can use to help students get feedback from peers during the revising process is the magic circle. The steps are as follows:

First, students identify a piece of writing for which they'd like a response (different from correcting mistakes or editing). Then the teacher collects students' writing papers. They should make sure that their name is not on the paper, or if it is that it is crossed out. It is important that students' writing be anonymous at this point. With younger students, move the desks in a circle facing inward. The teacher stands inside the circle and directs action.

Next, the teacher passes out a paper to each student. Students respond to that paper, letting the writer know what thoughts were going through their head as they read it. Students are to "think all over the paper" with their pencils. They should write on the paper, making marks and arrows to show exactly what they liked or wanted to know more about.

When students finish responding to a paper, they stand up, leave the paper on the desk, move to the center of the circle, and wait for an empty desk and respond to that paper. (Being able to get up and move around during the writing and responding process is helpful to many younger students who seem to have a hard time sitting still.) The goal should be to respond to at least three papers (this takes a lot of concentration—I would recommend doing sessions of five to ten minutes for younger primary age students, and ten to fifteen minutes for intermediate age students). With intermediate and middle school students, desks do not have to be moved into circles. When these students are finished responding to a paper they simply hold it in the air and trade with another student.

When you see the energy starting to lag, instruct students to finish the paper they are on and return it to a front table or spot that you have designated. When all papers are returned, students can then come up and find their own. They will find a paper that is alive with the thoughts and ideas of others.

This is a revising strategy, *not an editing strategy*. Getting real responses to writing makes it come alive and gives it energy. Revising is finished when students feel the writing is as they want it to be. Only then should they focus on editing, and not before. (Forgive me for overemphasizing this point. It's just that so much of the magic of writing is destroyed when it becomes a skills activity and not an expressive activity.) The steps and response guidelines for the magic circle are listed below:

Magic Circle

1. Collect papers (no names).

2. Put chairs in a circle.

3. Pass papers out.

4. Students respond to a paper (write on it).

5. When finished, leave it on the desk, move to center of the circle.

6. Wait for empty desk, respond to another paper.

7. Try to respond to at least three papers.

Response Guidelines

1. What did you like?

2. What did you want to know more about?

3. What might be added to make it more interesting?

4. What did it remind you of?

Editing

At the editing stage (different from the revising stage) students fix grammar, spelling, and punctuation errors. Two important points to reinforce at this stage: First, continue to reinforce the idea that good writing is not writing without errors. Good writing is having good ideas and then communicating them. Grammar, spelling, and punctuation are used to help students communicate their ideas. Second, let your students know that all writers need and use editors.

Self-editing. Teach students how to edit their own work by providing structure by using a simple checklist with three to five specific skills to look for (see the editing checklist below). As they edit have students focus on just one skill at a time. For example, they should first look to see that all sentences begin with capital letters and make a check in the "yes" column when they have done so. Then they should read each sentence out loud to see if it makes sense by itself and is a complete idea. When they have completed the editing checklist they should ask another student to review and edit their work.

Editing Checklist

1. Begins sentences with capital letters: yes _____ no _____

2. Writes sentences with a complete idea: yes _____ no _____

3. Ends sentences with a period: yes _____ no _____

4. Circles words that don't look
quite right (spelling):   yes _____ no _____

5. Uses "isn't" and "wasn't" correctly: yes _____ no _____

How do you handle words that don't quite look right? Students can look them up in the dictionary, or they can type the word into a word processor that has a spell check feature (of course, if they are doing their edits on the computer, they should use spell check and grammar check functions during their editing). There are also a variety of inexpensive electronic spelling dictionaries that can be purchased. (Interestingly enough, you can buy an electronic spelling dictionary for about the same price as a consumable spelling workbook.) Computer spell checks and electronic spelling dictionaries are both effective and efficient strategies to use when students are uncertain about the spelling of a word.

Peer editing: SET. Peer editing is a way for students to edit each other's papers. Editing other students' papers is also an indirect way to learn about spelling, grammar, and punctuation. SET stands for *skill expert tables.* The steps are as follows:

1. Designate a day or date for the editing of papers. Encourage students to have something ready to edit on that day. (For example, Fridays could be editing days.)

2. Identify three to eight skills related to grammar, spelling, or punctuation to focus on. Assign a table for each skill.

3. Assign students to tables and ask them to become experts in the use of that particular skill. For example, a spelling table would look just for spelling errors. Another table could be the sentence table looking for complete sentences with capital letters and periods. Another table could be the there/their and too/to/two table, checking to see that these are used correctly. Depending on your teaching or tutoring situation, assign two to five students to each editing table. Sometimes a parent volunteer, paraprofessional, or older student can be used to assist the work at each table. In these cases, they should intervene as little as possible. Real learning occurs when students discuss, communicate, and explain their thinking relative to a particular skill.

4. Each table examines and edits each paper looking only at their one particular editing element.

5. When a paper is finished at one table, it is passed to the next editing table until it completes all tables.

Peer editing: PET. PET stands for *professional editing tables*. The steps are as follows:

1. Designate one table for editing.

2. During the writing time, those who have completed revising their papers do an initial edit on their own.

3. When students have completed their own editing, they bring their pieces to the professional editing table (very much like professional writers do when they are finished with a piece of writing). Here a parent, paraprofessional, or older student works along with two or three voluntary editors. (Everyone in the class or tutoring group should have a chance to be an editor. This is one of the best ways to learn about grammar, spelling, and punctuation.)

4. Use a checklist to remind student editors of the things to look for. The checklist for PET below will give you a sense of what this might look like. Use students' papers to decide the specific elements to use in creating your own.

Checklist for PET
Things to Check
I. SENTENCES
    a. The writer uses complete sentences. ____
    b. The sentences are easy to read. ____
    c. The sentences use capital letters at the beginning and periods or ending marks at the end. ____
2. PARAGRAPHS
    a. Ideas are organized into paragraphs. ____
    b. Paragraphs are used to start a new idea. ____
    c. Paragraphs are indented at the beginning. ____
3. SPELLING
    a. The writer uses spell check on questionable words. ____
    b. Spells contractions correctly: isn't, wasn't, can't, didn't, they're. ____
    c. Uses there, their, and they're correctly. ____

If you are wondering what skills to teach students, look at their papers to see what types of errors seem to be reoccurring. Create short lessons to teach those skills explicitly. Then create a checklist including these skills in the editing process.

Publishing/Sharing

Publishing/sharing refers to any situation where students get eyeballs or ears on their writing. Having an audience respond to your writing makes it come alive. You're limited only by your imagination in how you might create an audience for students' work. Below eight strategies are described.

Author's chair. This is where a student reads a piece that she or he has written. If you are in a classroom setting, have one or two students sign up for author's chair each day. I have found that two students a day generally works best.

Student books. Students love to read each other's work. Create books for your classroom library that are made up of students' writing. This is done by having individual students collect their best writings and create a book. They would then design and illustrate a cover as well as create pictures that might be included with each story.

You can also create books comprised of more than one student's work. This multistudent book could be centered on a theme such as "Winter Stories" or "Funny Things" or it simply could be a collection of student stories. Select an editing team (just like real life), composed of three to six students. Its job is to work with a teacher, paraprofessional, parent, or older student to select stories, edit them, put them in a logical order, and create a structure along with a table of contents for the book. The editing team might also select students who are outstanding artists to illustrate the stories.

Student magazines or newspapers. Create a monthly magazine (or twice monthly) that contains student stories along with other articles found in magazines. You could have advice columns, editorials, comics, or information columns based on students' interests or expertise. Magazines and newspapers don't have to be limited to a single classroom. They can be gradewide or even schoolwide.

PowerPoint books. PowerPoint books enable students to copy and paste pictures from the Internet to create a visually pleasing story. You can also use digital pictures that you or students have taken, or you might scan

Figure 19.2.   Comic Strip Boxes

and use pictures that students have drawn. These pictures would be used to illustrate or enhance students' stories. Of course this works better for shorter stories than longer ones. The slide show function on PowerPoint enables students to have an electronic page turner. Students' stories could then be shown to the whole class or simply left on a computer for individual students.

An e-story.   A variation on the PowerPoint story is the e-story. This is simply a matter of copying and pasting Internet and digital pictures into a word processing document to illustrate or enhance the story. This works better for longer documents. These longer stories would then be printed and read.

Comic strips or comic books.   Similar to a PowerPoint book, students must think in visual images when creating a story. You can provide structure initially by giving students a blank comic strip form and letting them create stories around this (figure 19.2). Here students draw the pictures first and write dialogue or action later. The other way is to write the story first, then break it into picture boxes. Longer stories would require a page filled with comic strip boxes.

Bulletin board showcase.   This classic idea is still effective. Create a place on a bulletin board or wall for showcase stories. These are stories that have been edited and ones you believe to be outstanding in some respect. Encourage students to use pictures to illustrate or enhance their stories. These can also be placed outside the classroom in the hall or lunchroom for other students to read.

Online website.   For those of you savvy enough, create a website to display students' stories. Links can be used to organize stories by topic, date, or student.

Internet Search Terms

Writing, prewriting, and drafting: *writing-strategies-prewriting, writing-strategies-draft, teaching-writing-draft.*

Revising, editing, publishing: *peer-editing, peer-editing, peer-editing-activities, student-writing-revision, teaching-revision-strategies, teaching-writing-process, teaching-students-edit, writing-process-publishing, writing-process-publishing-ideas, elementary-students-publishing-web.*

References

Graves, D. (1983) *Writing: Teachers and children at work.* Portsmouth, N.H.: Heinemann.

AUTHENTIC WRITING AND WRITING PROMPTS

Authentic Writing

How much talking do you think young children would do if we corrected them after every utterance? What if we insisted that they pronounce every word perfectly and used only correct grammar as they were learning to speak? What if we assigned children their speaking topics and then corrected and evaluated their speaking instead of responding to their ideas? What do you think would happen? I can tell you: We'd create a generation of insecure, semipsychotic mutes.

And yet, this is what often happens when children are first learning to use the medium of writing as a vehicle for expressing their ideas. Well-meaning but ill-informed teachers or parents often insist that children's writing always be grammatically correct and error free as soon as it hits the paper. This is a good way to create reluctant or nonwriters. Just like learning to speak, the ability to write is developed best by sharing real ideas and getting real responses (versus constant correction) from adults and other students. Don't get me wrong here: Grammar, spelling, and punctuation are important, but these things are not writing. Writing is having ideas, organizing ideas, and communicating ideas. In this sense, grammar, spelling, and punctuation are a means to an end, but they are not ends by themselves.

Authentic Writing Activities

Learning to write is easier if students are engaged in authentic writing activities. Authentic writing activities are those in which students are asked to express their thoughts, share their ideas, or describe things from their lives or experience. Authentic writing comes from within the student. In this way also, every student can experience success. For example, if you ask a student to describe what he or she likes to do on weekends, every child can do this. Some may need to use more pictures than words, but every child can use print to create meaning.

Figure 20.1 shows examples of some early authentic writing. The writing is authentic because this is exactly what my nephews wanted to say to me. Nobody was directing them to write a story about frogs or princesses, or describe a day in the life of a shoe, or tell what they would wish for if they had three wishes. The motivation to communicate was internal. The writing expressed their ideas and came from their experiences. It was an authentic writing experience—the ultimate kind of writing.

The writing prompts below can be used to create more authentic writing experiences. Keep in mind that a writing prompt is only a temporary device (like one of those skinny spare tires used to get you to the next gas station when you have a flat tire). Ultimately, you want students to be able to choose their own writing topics (most of the time).

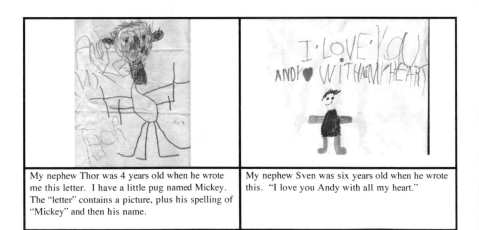

| My nephew Thor was 4 years old when he wrote me this letter. I have a little pug named Mickey. The "letter" contains a picture, plus his spelling of "Mickey" and then his name. | My nephew Sven was six years old when he wrote this. "I love you Andy with all my heart." |

Figure 20.1. Examples of Early Authentic Writing

Internal Writing Prompts (these are good)

1. Tell me about a time . . .

2. What do you think about . . .

3. Describe . . .

4. Tell me about . . .

5. What do you think is interesting about . . .

6. What do you want to know about . . .

7. What do you think about . . .

8. What do you want to tell . . .

9. What do you want to say to . . .

10. What do you want to say?

11. What did you see when . . .

12. What did you think when . . .

13. Describe a time when you . . .

14. Describe a time when . . .

15. I need to remember to . . .

16. I wish that I . . .

The Internet search terms at the end of the chapter will provide you with literally thousands of writing prompts at your fingertips. As always, adopt and adapt to meet the needs of your students.

Functional Writing

Functional writing (the type of writing done for everyday sorts of tasks) can be used to design authentic writing activities. Six functional writing tasks are described below.

Letters to parents, grandparents, or other relatives.   Have students write simple, short letters telling about something at school, a tutoring session, or something else going on in students' lives. Relatives love getting cards.

Cards for holidays or special occasions. Students can make simple holiday cards or greeting cards. The easiest way is to cut a 6x11 paper in half and then fold it. You could also make up holidays or special occasions such as "Happy Haircut" or "Happy New Shoes." Have students illustrate or decorate their cards as well.

Rules. Students create and write a set of rules for reading class (three to five) to be posted. Rules may include such things as: try your best, find books that you like, always bring your notebook, and so on.

Lists or things to remember. Students create lists of things or important events they need to remember. This could be used to remember things scheduled for that day. A planner or calendar could also be used to remember things more long term.

Reading lists. In a portfolio, journal, or on a poster, students keep a list of books (and other things) they have read.

Journals. Using journals or literature logs can be used to record students' reactions to what they are reading or for any of the aesthetic response questions and activities described in chapter 15.

Inauthentic Writing Activities

Inauthentic writing activities are those in which students are asked to express other people's ideas, to write things that they don't necessarily want to say, or to use writing to organize or explain somebody else's thoughts or experiences. This occurs when students are asked to write a report on a subject somebody else has chosen for them or to do a book report in order to prove that they've read the book. Often these types of writing activities are used as a measuring device (purely to assign a grade), or to make students demonstrate that they've read the assigned story or text. Below are some examples of the kinds of writing prompts that can lead to inauthentic writing experiences.

External Writing Prompts (these are not so good)

1. Write a story about . . .

2. Describe the part in the story where . . .

3. What is the author's point of view . . .

4. Write a report on . . .

5. What was the character's reaction when . . .

Thus said, there are times and places when it's appropriate to use the types of external writing activities and assignments described above. The problem with external writing prompts is that they often become the *only* type of writing that students are asked to do in schools. Nobody asks students what they think or what they want to say. Nobody encourages them to wonder. They're not asked to use writing to organize their thoughts, to describe their experiences, or to express their reactions to a particular event. When students' writing is based solely on external prompts, the motivation also becomes external. Their writing does not come from a natural desire to express or say what they want to say. This makes writing and learning to write much harder for students, especially those who may be less proficient in the first place. (It also makes it much more difficult to teach.) We want to make learning to read and write as easy as possible.

Stories

What about writing stories? Would it be motivating to ask students to write stories? When in your adult life have you been asked to write a story about something?

"Write a story about a magic wizard and a lost student . . ." "Write a story about a donkey and a flying monkey . . ." "Write a story about a boy who lost his three-pronged electrical adaptor and . . ."

Unless you are an author of novels or children's books, I would guess the number of times this has occurred in your life would be about . . . never. Thus, the writing of imaginative stories should be put in perspective.

There is an important place for creative writing. They can be a marvelous outlet for expressing ideas and feelings; however, literacy instruction should also reflect and include what occurs most often in real life. In real life, adults are commonly asked to organize and describe their thoughts. We write memos, letters, lists, newspaper articles, letters-to-the-editor, and yes, e-mail. Very seldom are we asked to write stories. Thus, to prepare children for real life, we should replicate reality in our instruction at the level that is most appropriate to students' level of intellectual and emotional development.

Again, I am not saying that you should never encourage creative writing and imaginative stories. Nor am I advocating that creative story prompts should never be used (use whatever gets students writing). What I am saying is that external writing prompts that call for once-upon-a-time stories can be abstract, making writing more difficult. Instead, try to get children to write from their experiences or expectations. "What did you do? What did you see? What do you think? What do you do when . . . What makes you feel . . ." In this way their "stories" are really their stories. That is, stories in which they are the central character.

More Is Not Better

Have you ever run into somebody who had absolutely nothing to say, but said it anyway? Have you ever encountered writing that seemed to serve no other purpose than to fill the page with words? How often in your adult life has somebody told you to go back and rewrite something to make it more interesting or to add more to it? I would guess again about . . . never. In our real adult worlds, being able to writing concisely and express our ideas using as few words as possible generally means that the things we write will be read. (Nobody likes to read long rambling letters or textbooks.) Thus, when children complete their writing, very seldom should they be asked to go back and write a little more, or to add more to it. When students say what needs to be said, encourage them to go on to their next piece of writing and say something else.

I can see the question forming in your head: What if students write the absolute minimum? Well then, have them write more absolute minimums. Not more of, but more. Instead of asking them to tell you more about something they've said quite enough about, ask them to tell you about other things. Remember: rigor is not the same as complexity. Quality is not the same as quantity. Shorter writing activities are just fine.

Writing Prompts for Primary Age Students

Primary age students tend to experience the world in very concrete terms. For the most part, they have yet to develop abstract reasoning abilities.

Thus, their writing prompts need to be concrete yet open-ended. Their writing prompts should invite them to describe their specific experiences, feelings, ideas, or perceptions. These prompts should enable students to say what they wanted to say in the first place. In this way, the writing and the motivation are internal and intrinsic.

Unfinished Sentences

So the trick, when using a writing prompt for any age student, is to provide just enough assistance to get students writing—but not so much as to interfere with the natural writing process. Unfinished sentences can be used to this end. Below are some examples of unfinished sentences.

Unfinished Sentences

1. On the way to school today I saw . . .

2. I really like to . . .

3. _____ is something I do when I'm bored.

4. I had a really fun time when . . .

5. It was scary.

6. It was fun.

7. I couldn't believe that . . .

8. This makes me happy.

9. I wish . . .

10. I get angry when . . .

11. I am very proud of . . .

12. When I'm feeling sad I . . .

13. When I'm feeling happy I . . .

14. Yesterday I . . .

15. Tomorrow I will . . .

16. I remember when . . .

Other Writing Prompts or Ideas

Here are three prompts for creating your own writing prompts.

Notice. What did you notice? What did you see or hear on the way to school?

Do. What did you do? What did you do at recess? What did you do over the weekend? What did you do after school?

Draw. Draw a picture of something interesting you saw or did. Use words to explain the picture.

Remember: Your goal should be to create the situation where writing prompts are not needed. You want students begin to notice, imagine, and think and write from internal prompts.

Internet Search Terms

Writing prompts: *writing-prompts, primary-writing-prompts, elementary-writing-prompts, student-writing-prompts, writing-prompts-unfinished-sentences, creative-writing-prompts, authentic-writing-prompts, ideas-for-student-writing.*

CHAPTER TWENTY-ONE

TEMPORARY SPELLING AND ASSESSING SUCCESS IN WRITING

Temporary Spelling

This question often arises: Should you insist on correct spelling when children are getting their initial ideas on paper? Short answer: no.

Real writers edit last. There's a time and a place to look at spelling, grammar, and punctuation errors: in the editing stage (the five-step writing process is described below). We want students to view their writing as a way to capture and express their ideas. Overemphasizing conventional spelling in the beginning stages can inhibit writing. This reflects what happens in the real world where initial drafts are messy things with lots of spelling and grammar errors. In the writing of this book, my initial drafts had lots of errors (less so because I have grammar and spell check). The point is that we should treat our students just as real writers are treated. Real writers have messy first drafts and revisions. They edit during the final phases of their writing.

Good writing is writing that expresses ideas efficiently and effectively. Good writing is different from error-free writing. Attending to the mechanics of writing is very important, but it must occur in the appropriate place in the appropriate way. Indeed, spelling, punctuation, and grammar should be seen by students as elements the help them transmit their message more effectively. Errors in any one of these areas will dilute or diffuse the message. Editing of spelling, grammar, and punctuation should occur near the end of the writing process, after a piece has been revised many times. This enables students to see editing in the context of effectively delivering their message.

Temporary spelling enhances the flow of ideas.   When students are writing and they ask how to spell a word, tell them to use as many letters as they can hear to hold the idea. This is called temporary spelling, a placeholder for the idea. You might want to have students underline their temporary spelling so that they'll know which words to give attention to during the editing phase of their writing.

Learning to spell is a developmental process.   Won't children learn the incorrect spelling if they are allowed to use temporary spelling to hold the idea? No. Learning to spell, like learning to talk, is a developmental process. We proceed through a series of stages until we become mature talkers or spellers (Gentry, 2006). There is very little correlation between the use of temporary spelling and students' performance on spelling tests. There is some evidence to support the idea that the use of temporary spelling will speed students' development or process through the various stages (Manning & Underbakke, 2005).

Teachers need to model temporary spelling.   Students often feel reluctant at first to have a go at unknown words (especially low achieving students). They don't want to be seen as doing something wrong. You must create the conditions whereby temporary spelling is acceptable. This can be done by composing in front of students, thinking out loud as you do so. When doing this, use a word you may not know how to spell (even if you have to pretend you don't know how to spell it), and tell students, "I'm not quite sure how to spell this word, so I'm going to just use a few letters to hold the idea. I'll come back to this one later."

Temporary spelling enables success.   Temporary spelling enables teachers to recognize and value students' ideas. It also provides a venue for low achieving readers and writers to experience success. Often students who have reading difficulties experience nothing but failure for the entire time they are in the classroom. Is it any wonder that they sometimes act out? Earning success can contribute to students' overall academic achievement. Success contributes to positive self-esteem. Self-esteem is highly correlated with students' achievement (Woolfolk, 2007). This doesn't mean that high self-esteem necessarily causes high achievement—just that the two are strongly related.

Temporary spelling improves phonemic and phonetic awareness. Temporary spelling improves children's ability to hear letter sounds within words (Martins & Silva, 2003). This is called phonemic awareness. It also improves their ability to make connections between letters and sounds. This is called phonetic awareness. These are both important prerequisite skills in learning to read. By listening for sounds and using as many letters as they can to hold their ideas during the writing process, students become better able to hear and make letter sound relationships.

Specific strategies related to spelling instruction are described in the next chapter.

Assessing Writing Success

Assessment of any kind should inform our instruction. That is, we assess to see how students are doing, to see how well we're teaching, and to get a sense of what skills need to be taught. The writing assessment form (WAF) can be used to document students' growth while inviting them to experience success.

Writing Assessment Form
Writing prompt or topic:

Key: 4 = outstanding, 3 = very good, 2 = average, 1 = low
- Content, ideas: _____
- Mechanics (spelling, grammar, punctuation): _____
- Met deadlines, fulfilled assignment requirements: _____
- Organization, structure: _____
- Fluency, communication: _____
- Appearance: _____

Ideas or insights:

Skills to work on:

It's important to describe struggling readers and writers in terms of what they can do instead of only describing what they can't do or how far they are away from the mythical average. The rating checklist below can be used to point out a few things for students to work on while providing areas in which they may experience success even though they may struggle with spelling, grammar, or punctuation skills (good ideas, meets deadline, strong organization).

Rating Checklist

Key: 4 = outstanding, 3 = very good, 2 = average, 1 = low

- Organization: _____
- Sentences, sentence structure: _____
- Interest, ideas: _____
- Grammar: _____
- Spelling and punctuation: _____
- Effective communication: _____
- Meets deadline: _____

Notes/things to remember:

The writing checklist below can be used to help students edit their writing and as a form of assessment. Each of these types of assessment should be adopted and adapted to meet the particular needs and interests of you and your students. It is best to focus on only two to four skills at a time. It's important to include at least two areas in which students can experience success unrelated to writing mechanics

CHECKLIST OF SKILLS TAUGHT

Skill	Dates			
	2/11	2/21	2/27	
CAPITALIZATION				
Names of people	I	L	L	M
Cities and towns				
States				
Countries				
Street names			I	L
Titles				
Days				
Months				
Holidays				

Key: I – introduced, L - learning , M- mastered

CHECKLIST OF SKILLS TAUGHT

Student: _____

Key: √ = trait is present, √- = trait is present sometimes, # = oops

Skill	Dates			
	4/11	4/17	4/23	
SENTENCES				
Uses complete sentences	√-	√	√	
Capitalizes beginning word	√	√	√	
Puts period at the end	#	√-	√	
PARAGRAPHS				
Contains a set of related ideas	#	√-	√-	
Starts a new paragraph with a new ideas	#	√-	√	
Indents	√	√	√	

Figure 21.1.   Checklists

Writing Checklist
Key: ✓ = trait is present; ✓– = trait is present sometimes; # = oops

- Uses complete sentences: _____
- Separates ideas by paragraph: _____
- Capitalizes first letter in sentence: _____
- Puts periods at the ends of sentences: _____
- Capitalizes names: _____
- Uses prewriting strategy: _____
- Revises: _____
- Peer edits: _____
- Uses spell check: _____
- Uses grammar check: _____.
- Has interesting ideas: _____
- Communicates effectively: _____

Things done well:

Specific skills to work on next time:

A checklist can also be used to document what and when you have taught specific skills and the level at which students have grasped them. The checklist on the bottom of figure 21.1 can be used for individual students to document the appearance of writing skills in their writing.

Word of caution: In your Internet search you will discover that temporary or invented spelling seems to generate a great deal of emotion and angst by those outside the literacy community. You will find a great deal of hyperbole used to describe why temporary spelling is a bad thing. You might even (as I did) come across those who see temporary spelling and whole language as some sort of conspiracy. You can be sure that these types of claims and rants are made by those who have not taken the time to examine the body of research related to spelling and literacy instruction.

Internet Search Terms

Temporary spelling: *spelling-temporary, spelling-invented, spelling-strategies-temporary, writing-temporary-spelling, teaching-temporary-spelling, using-temporary-spelling, lessons-temporary-spelling.*

Assessment: *writing-authentic-assessment, writing-assessment, writing-direct-assessment, writing-assessment-rubric, writing-assessment-checklist, student-writing-checklist.*

References

Gentry, R. (2006) *Breaking the code: The new science of reading and writing.* Portsmouth, N.H.: Heinemann.

Graves, D. (1983) *Writing: Teachers and children at work.* Portsmouth, N.H.: Heinemann.

Manning, M., & Underbakke, C. (2005) Spelling development research necessitates replacement of weekly word list. *Childhood Education, 81,* 236–39.

Martins, M. A., & Silva, C. (2003) Relations between children's invented spelling and the development of phonological awareness. *Educational Psychology, 23,* 4–16.

Woolfolk, A. (2007) *Educational psychology* (tenth ed.). Boston: Allyn and Bacon.

WORD CLASS: A MORE EFFECTIVE APPROACH TO SPELLING INSTRUCTION

W eekly spelling tests have been the staple of elementary education for the last one hundred years. Here students memorize a list of words each week and then take a test on Friday. Tests are corrected, scores are taken, and one is deemed either a good speller or not a good speller. This would be a great way to teach spelling except for one thing: it's not very effective. Studying a list of words out of any meaningful context has minimal effect in helping to develop students' spelling proficiency, and worse, it keeps students away from real writing experiences (Gentry & Gilbert, 1993; Graves, 1983). This chapter describes a better way to help students learn how to spell correctly in authentic writing conditions (Johnson, 1998).

Spelling Proficiency and Visual Memory

What is the difference between a good speller and a poor speller? According to Gentry (2006), spelling proficiency might be attributed to one's visual memory capacity. That is, good spellers are better able to store and retrieve necessary letter patterns from their long-term memory than less able spellers. Effective spelling instruction then should focus on improving the efficiency of this storage and retrieval. This can be done by using activities and assignments that help students become more aware of letter patterns and word parts.

Word Class Approach

Word class is an approach to spelling instruction that I designed several years ago (Johnson, 1998). This is an approach that meets the special needs of both high ability and low ability spellers. Here students select the words they wish to study each week. Sounds crazy I know, but read on.

Choice

Allowing students to choose the books they want to read and their writing topics is a powerful motivator in reading and writing. (Imagine if, in your adult life, somebody else always chose the books that you would read for pleasure.) Choice of spelling words is equally motivating. Word class teaches students how to generate and choose the words they will study each week. Choice here doesn't mean total choice all the time, however. This choice might happen in one of three forms:

Choice within a topic or category. Given a topic, students create their own spelling lists. For example, if you were studying the rainforest in a science or social studies class, students would be able to generate and choose a list of related words. Words could also be taken from a book students are reading or from current events. Spelling can then be used to reinforce concepts taught in other subject areas. Students are also able to see their spelling words in places other than the list in their spelling books.

Choice within their lives or experiences. This is sometimes call total choice. Here students use their lives and experience to create their own spelling lists. This approach is usually the most interesting, as children search their lives for interesting and meaningful words.

Choice with a spelling pattern. While this is the least desirable of the three choice options, there are times when it is appropriate to generate a list of words around a spelling pattern. Here, the teacher begins with a short mini-lesson covering a particular spelling pattern or skill.

Generating Spelling Lists

In word class, each student studies a personalized list of words each week. This list can be generated in large group or small group.

Large group. Initially, words for spelling lists should be generated in large group. This enables students to see many words and choose the ones that are of interest or importance to them. Given a topic or category, start by providing a couple of examples of words within that category to prime the pump. Then ask students to think of other words to be included. These words are written on the board. (Seeing words gives students ideas for other words.) After a large number of words have been generated, students would choose eight to ten words to study during the week (give them a specific number). Advise them to check the spelling of the words, as you may not have spelled them correctly.

Pairs or small group. You can make this a cooperative learning activity by defining a specific task and then creating roles. The group's task is to generate thirty words for spelling lists (more or less depending on age and ability). Each student within the group then chooses ten words from the group's list to study that week. With primary students use groups of three or four. With intermediate and middle school students, use groups of four to six. Some or all of the following roles can be used:

President: makes final decisions, assigns roles.

Scribe: records words.

Spell checker: uses a dictionary, word processor, or electronic spell checker to insure the correct spelling.

Brain: thinks up words. (You may want to have more than one person here.)

Sociologist: makes sure everyone contributes an idea.

Investigator: looks in books, magazines, or the Internet for words related to the topic. (You may want to have more than one person here.)

Spelling word sign-up. Put a large poster made of butcher paper on a bulletin board or taped to the wall with the next week's spelling topic. Below are some examples of spelling word sign-up posters related to the three types of choice. Put a pencil or marker on a string next to the poster. Encourage students to think of and write interesting or important words.

Spelling Word Sign-Up Posters
Next Week's Spelling Words—**Water Resources**

Please add interesting or important words.

Next Week's Spelling Words—**Your Life**

Please add interesting or important words.

Next Week's Spelling Words—**Words with EA**

Please add interesting or important words.

Selecting Words—Multilevel

But what if students just pick easy words? Well, then they would be able to experience much-needed success. This is a good thing. However, Topping (1995) found that the words students choose are usually longer and more complex than those chosen by teachers. This is because they choose words of interest to them regardless of the complexity or length.

To ensure that students are exposed to words of varying difficulty levels, you can choose to include two to five mandatory words for all students to study each week. To make this multilevel, assign different mandatory words for specific students. In doing this, don't make the mistake of giving high ability spellers more words to study. Instead, assign more complex words for higher-level spellers, less complex words for struggling spellers. These would be written out on a 3x5 inch card and given to students after they have identified the words for their individual word lists.

Word Book

Students' individual word lists should be recorded in their personal word books. The word book is like a journal or learning log. It should be kept on a shelf or some other special place other than students' desks. This will ensure that it doesn't get lost or become something to tear paper out of for use on other assignments. Keeping the word books on a shelf also enables you to quickly go through them as a form of formative assessment, and to make comments and respond to them, creating a dialogue journal.

The word book will be used throughout the week for various writing activities using the list words (see below). You are limited only by your imagination here in the types of activities and writing experiences you design. The goal however is to get students to use their list words and to recognize or manipulate letter patterns. The word book is to be used in place of the expensive consumable spelling books, which are of little use when teaching students how to spell.

Documenting Growth—Celebrating Learning

On Fridays you'll still give a spelling test (we call them celebrations of learning); however, instead of giving the same test to all your students, each will be taking his or her own individualized test. To do this, students pair up with a buddy. The first student hands the second student his or her lists of spelling words. The second student then reads the words (administers the test) while the first takes the test. After the first test has been taken and corrected, students change roles.

After both tests, students record their results in their word books or portfolios. A line graph or bar graph can be used to provide a visual reference (figure 22.1).

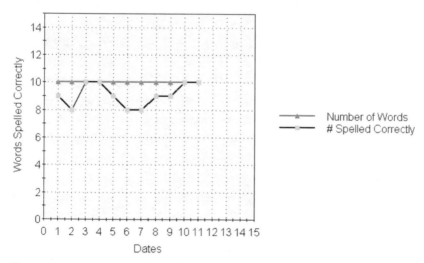

Figure 22.1. Graph for Word Class

Direct Assessment of Spelling

In your real life how is your spelling assessed? That is, how do people know if you're a good or a poor speller? Answer: They look at your writing. An authentic form of spelling assessment would be WPH (words per hundred) scores. Here, the teacher examines a student's final edited draft, designates a hundred-word segment, and then counts the number of words spelled correctly in that one-hundred-word segment to arrive at a WPH score. This evaluates students' ability to spell (and edit) under authentic writing conditions. Also, this is how real writers' spelling ability is evaluated in the real world. With younger students, a WPF score (words per fifty) or even a WPTF score (words per twenty-five) can be used.

Advantages of Word Class

There are four advantages of using the self-selected words approach:

Students' ideas and experiences are valued. By their choice, students are invited to bring their world and experiences into their literacy class. They select words that they are interested in. This creates a strong connection between school life and real life and provides greater motivation to read and write.

More time can be spent doing real writing. The goal of language arts instruction is not to fill out spelling books or to pass grammar tests (although spelling and grammar are both important). The goal of language arts class is to enable students to *use the language*. We want our students to be able to write effectively. Too much time spent drilling spelling, grammar, and punctuation subskills can get in the way of authentic writing experiences. Instruction in these areas is very important, but it should be kept short and quickly paced so that students can get to the business of writing. Also, students' own writing provides the best context for learning these skills.

Money spent on consumable spelling books can be used to buy real books, or paper and pencils. Consumable spelling books cost anywhere from $14 to $25. Imagine how many good books you could buy for that price. In a classroom, this money could provide the basis of a nice classroom library. (It is important to have exciting, interesting, new books for children to read—both at home and at school. How do we expect children to read if we provide nothing of interest for them to do so?)

Students develop depth and dimension to their word knowledge. As you'll see below, the activities used in word class will expand students' knowledge of particular words. Since students select words that interest them, the activities are more likely to move these words into their productive vocabulary (they use them in their own speaking and writing).

Word Class Activities

Spelling instruction should be limited to about twenty minutes a day (Gentry & Gilbert, 1993). This section describes a variety of activities that can be used during this time. These activities add depth and dimension to word knowledge, highlight letter patterns, enhance writing skills, and value students' ideas and experiences.

Word walls. A word wall (Cunningham & Allington, 1994) can be used to call attention to interesting or important words within the given topic or spelling pattern. This strategy was described in an earlier chapter.

Word sorts. Students sort their words by creating groups. A group is one or more things that are the same. These groups could be related to spelling patterns (and letters) or ideas. Word sorts can be recorded in students' word books. With a little imagination, they can also be incorporated into art projects. Here are some examples of spelling pattern groups and idea groups:

Spelling Pattern Groups
List: dock, fish, swim, boat, water-ski, jump, life jacket, soggy, cold, dip, diving board
1. **Short "i" group:** swim, fish, dip
2. **"Ck" group:** dock, life jacket
3. **Consonant blend group:** fish, swim, water-ski, diving board, jump
4. **Two-word group:** water-ski, life jacket, diving board
5. **One-syllable group:** dock, fish, swim, boat, cold, dip

Idea Groups
List: dock, fish, swim, boat, water-ski, jump, life jacket, soggy, cold, dip, diving board
1. **Water-ski group:** boat, water-ski, life jacket, soggy
2. **Swimming group:** swim, jump, cold, diving board, dip

3. **Fishing group:** dock, fish, boat

4. **Doing group:** fish, swim, water-ski, jump, dip

Crossword puzzles. Do an Internet search using the search terms found at the end of this chapter. There are many free programs that enable students to create their own crossword puzzles (www.crosswordpuzzlegames.com/create.html). These puzzles invite students to focus on letter patterns, as each letter must correspond to a box, as well as word meaning. Also, plain old graph paper with one-inch or half-inch boxes works just as well. Students should create these puzzles for other students to do. For struggling students, a word box with the answers can be included with the crossword puzzle.

Word box riddles. Word box riddles invite students to focus on meaning and letter patterns of words. Here a line is used to hold each letter of the riddle answer. Some riddles may include one or more letter clues. Just like crossword puzzles, students should create these puzzles for other students to do. Again, word boxes containing the answers can be included for those who may have difficulty (see below).

Word Box Riddles

1. I hate when my corn flakes are this: _ _ _ _ _.

2. I row, row, row this: _ _ _ _.

3. A very quick swim: _ _ p.

4. Dolphins can do this very well: S _ _ _.

5. **Word box:** dock, fish, swim, boat, water-ski, jump, life jacket, soggy, cold, dip, diving board.

Super Word Web. A Super Word Web (SWW) was described in chapter 12. Here students see a word in the context of a sentence. They're then asked to generate synonyms and associations. This activity should be done in small groups or pairs. You may have students work with a partner during one day's spelling activities. Here they would each create two SWWs based on their spelling words. These could be written in their word books or they could create posters to hang up on the walls.

Write a sentence. Using words from their personalized lists, students can experiment with words and ideas by writing different kinds of sentences in their word books. Some ideas for sentences are listed below:

Write . . .
a spooky sentence.
a silly sentence.
a big sentence.
a sentence using two of your words.
a tiny sentence.
a blue sentence.
a wild sentence.
a boring sentence.
a sentence about your day.
a sentence using exactly seven words.
a sentence using exactly three words.
a very long sentence.
a sentence about you.
a sentence using three of your words.
a sentence using none of your words.
a nonsense sentence.
a sentence about something important.
a sentence about your week.

Word association paragraph (WAP). Students pick one of the words from their personalized lists, then think of three to six things related to or associated with their list words (you may need to model this). Students then use the word and associations to create sentences or paragraphs to create a WAP (below). They do not have to use all their words in the sentences or paragraphs they create.

WAP
Word: soggy.
Associations: cornflakes, crisp, milk, morning, Frosted Flakes, crunchy.
Paragraph: I love to eat my cornflakes when they're crunchy like fall leaves. I hate when people call me on the phone in the

middle of eating. I'm worried that my cornflakes will get soggy. It's funny because they still taste the same. It's just that it feels different.

WAP
Word: soggy.
Associations: rain, raining, mud, boots, wet clothes, school, yellow raincoat, hate, school, soak.
Paragraph: I remember going to school when I was in first grade when it was raining. It was soaking wet. I wore a yellow raincoat with a hat. The raincoats back then were pretty stiff and heavy. I loved the smell of them. I'd wear it with my heavy, black buckle boots. They kept my feet from getting soggy.

Life connection.   Students select a list word, then use it to describe something happening in their lives or something that has happened. For example, if they included the word "swim," they might describe a particular swimming episode or what they do when they go swimming.

Treasure hunt.   Students look in their textbooks, reading books, or other written material for words. There are four kinds of treasure hunts: (a) look for words from their list words, (b) pick a word and look for synonyms or similar phrases, (c) pick a word and look for associations or related words (students must explain the connection), or (d) pick a word and look for similar spelling patterns (*spelling patterns, word families, endings, beginnings, middles*).

Webbing to write story paragraphs.   Students use webbing as a prewriting strategy (see figure 22.2) to create a story paragraph based on one or more spelling words. The web provides structure for a piece of writing. Ideally these story paragraphs are related to some part of students' personal lives or experience. At the end of the lesson, students record their best or most interesting pieces of writing in their word journals.

Webbing to write information.   Webbing to write information (expository text) is a bit different from webbing to write stories (figure 22.2). Here the student is telling something or explaining. Webs are effective in teaching the concept of a paragraph. Each node (a group of ideas) becomes a paragraph.

WEBBING TO WRITE STORIES.

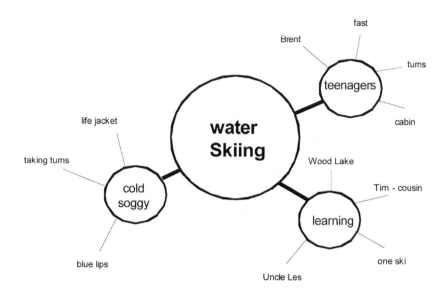

WEBBING TO WRITE INFORMATION

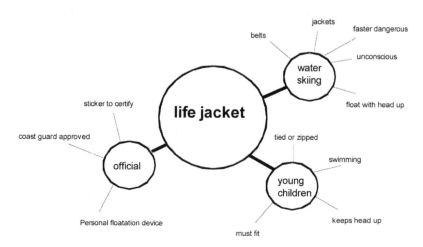

Figure 22.2.   Webbing

Webbing to speak. Students pick a word from their spelling lists to use in creating short one-minute oral presentations in small group. Here students identify a topic (the topic could be a spelling list word or a related topic). Just like the web in figure 22.2, the topic name is put in the center of the web. Students are asked to think of two or three things about their topics that they think are important. These become the titles for the nodes. Students then brainstorm ideas for each node.

Instead of the large group speeches, which can be frightening (and a little boring), students are put into small groups of three to six students. One student stands and delivers the speech using the web as a guide to his or her speech. One person in the group should be the timer. With younger students, these speeches should be about thirty seconds. With older students, speeches should be one to two minutes. For more information on using oral communication across the curriculum, see *Making Connections in Elementary and Middle School Social Studies* (Johnson, 2006). The small group format enables students to practice oral communication in smaller, more comfortable settings. It also enables the teacher to watch several speeches simultaneously as students in several groups will be speaking at the same time (this was described in greater depth in chapter 19).

Webbing to find related word parts. Here, students web to find related parts of a word. Students choose a word from their spelling lists and break it into beginning, middle, and ending parts. For example the word, "jump" can be broken into three parts: "j" beginning, short "u" middle, and "mp" blend for the ending (figure 22.3). The word "jump" is the central idea. "j," "u," and "mp" are the three nodes. With a partner, students brainstorm on

Figure 22.3. Webbing for Related Word Parts

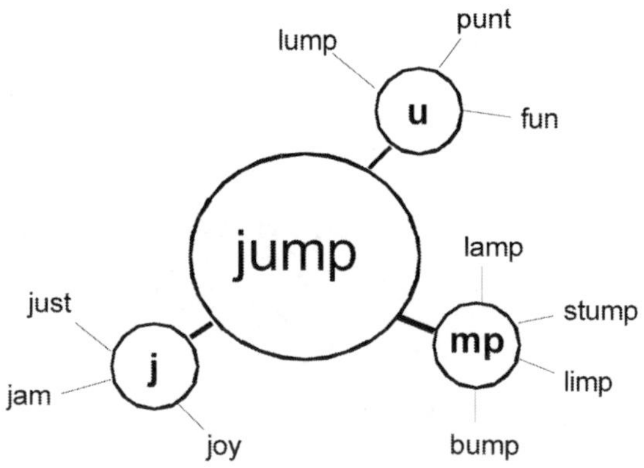

each node to find words with similar parts. The web is recorded in students' word journals.

Internet Search Terms

Crossword puzzles: *create-crossword-puzzle, crossword-puzzle-classroom, crossword-puzzle-kid, crossword-puzzle-maker, crossword-puzzle-spelling.*

Word search puzzles: *word-search-spelling, word-search-making, word-search-create, puzzle-maker-word-list, word-find-create, word-search-puzzle.*

Spelling activities: *spelling-ideas-activities, spelling-activities, spelling-games, spelling-words-lesson, spelling-games, spelling-best-practice.*

Assessment: *spelling-assessment, spelling-authentic-assessment, spelling-assessment-best-practice, spelling-inventories, spelling-inventory.*

References

Bartch, J. (1992) An alternative to spelling: An integrated approach. *Language Arts, 69,* 404–8.

Cunningham, P. M., & Allington, R. L. (1994).*Classrooms that work: They can all read and write.* New York: HarperCollins.

Gentry, R. (2006) *Breaking the code: The new science of beginning reading and writing.* Portsmouth, N.H.: Heinemann.

Gentry, R., & Gilbert, J. W. (1993) *Teaching kids to spell.* Portsmouth, N.H.: Heinemann.

Graves, D. (1983) *Writing: Teachers and children at work.* Portsmouth, N.H.: Heinemann.

Johnson, A. (1996) Inference: A thinking skill to enhance learning and literacy. *Wisconsin State Reading Association Journal, 40,* 9–13.

Johnson, A. (1998) Word class: A way to modify spelling instruction for gifted learners. *The Roeper Review, 20,* 128–131.

Johnson, A. (2006) *Making connections in elementary and middle school social studies.* Thousand Oaks, Calif.: SAGE Publications.

Topping, K. (1995) Cued spelling: A powerful technique for parent and peer tutoring. *The Reading Teacher, 48,* 374–85.1

LEARNING ABOUT GRAMMAR DOESN'T HAVE TO BE BORING AND MEANINGLESS

As the title suggests, learning about grammar doesn't have to be boring and meaningless. This chapter starts by dispelling some myths, otherwise known as silly grammar ideas. It ends by describing seven activities that can be used to develop students' ability to use conventional grammar.

Silly Grammar Ideas

The word *grammar* can send shudders up and down the spine of most middle school students. Why is that? Perhaps it is because of some of the myths or silly ideas that have been perpetuated around grammar. Seven silly grammar ideas are listed here.

Silly grammar idea #1: In order to be effective, grammar instruction has to be boring and meaningless. Truth: Not.

Silly grammar idea #2: In order to be able to write, students must be able to identify and define grammar subentities such as a pronoun, gerund, participle, superlative, relative clause, coordinating conjunction, causative verb, past participle, intransitive verb, ergative verb, imperative, intransitive verb, dangling modifier, predicate, past participle, transitive verb, prepositional phrase, reflexive pronoun. Truth: Knowledge of grammar is but one component of being able to write. Knowledge of grammar is important; however, knowing the five-step writing process, being able to use a grammar check on a computer, and knowing how get editing help from others is more important.

Silly grammar idea #3: If students have trouble writing, they just need a little more grammar instruction. Truth: Sometimes an overemphasis on writing subskills makes it more difficult to write. This is because, instead of seeing writing holistically or in a global sense, it becomes perceived as a complex myriad of little subskills

Silly grammar idea #4: There is a correlation between students' knowledge of grammar and the quality of their compositions. Truth: There is little relationship between the teaching of grammar and the quality of students' written compositions.

Silly grammar idea #5: You must be an expert grammarian to be a good writer. Truth: If this were the case, grammarians would be our bestselling authors and always win the Pulitzer Prize.

Silly grammar idea #6: Studying grammar outside a meaningful writing context (doing grammar exercises in a book) improves students' ability to use grammar correctly in authentic writing situations. Truth: Studying grammar outside the context of authentic writing actually makes it more difficult to transfer these skills.

Silly grammar idea #7: You can teach writing and grammar without being a writer. Truth: All teachers of writing must write and share their writing with students. Would you take piano lessons from somebody who never played the piano?

For a quick overview of some research-based facts on the teaching of grammar, see www.boyntoncook.com/shared/onlineresources/08894/08894f5.html.

Grammar Instruction

Grammar is a study of how our language works. Learning to use certain conventions of grammar enables us to effectively create and transmit ideas from our heads out into the world through our writing and speaking. Traditional grammar instruction was very prescriptive (see stand-alone approach below). That is, it would prescribe what you must do or should do with the expectation that you would be able to transfer these ideas directly to your writing and speaking.

While, on the face of it, this seems to make sense, let me ask you this: How did you learn the basic grammar rules for speaking? Were you drilled in elements of grammar apart from any meaningful speaking context? I don't think so. You learned to speak and you acquired the basic rules of grammar by speaking and getting responses to your ideas, by hearing other more mature speakers, and by having incorrect grammar attended to in the context of your authentic speaking activities.

Grammar instruction is important; however, time spent composing has a more positive effect on grammar and writing than time spent teaching grammar (Hillocks, 1986). This means that grammar instruction must be short and explicit, and then practiced, and reviewed in authentic writing experiences. In this sense, writing and speaking are skills that are developed, not content to be taught.

Approaches to Grammar Instruction

There are three common approaches taken to the teaching of grammar.

Stand-alone approach or isolated approach. Grammar instruction is done as a separate class apart from any real reading or writing through the use of worksheets and/or artificial activities and assignments. In the 1970s, we did a lot of sentence diagramming. While there is a place for an occasional worksheet, this is not a very effective approach to helping students develop their ability to use grammar knowledge. There is very little transfer to real-life writing situations.

Immersion approach. Here students are immersed in real-life writing and reading situations. This immersion is an important aspect of helping to develop mature readers and writers; however, without instruction learning is not very efficient or effective.

Embedded approach. This is the most effective approach to grammar instruction. The teacher looks at students' papers to see what types of errors they're making. Based on his/her observation, skills are selected for short mini-lessons or coaching sessions. This is a very direct approach to grammar instruction as students are being given explicit and direct instruction on those aspects they are using in their authentic writing.

Elements of Effective Skills Instruction

The elements of effective skills instruction (Pressley, Harris, & Marks, 1992) were described in chapter 13. These should also be used with the teaching of grammar as well; however, instruction should be brief and quickly paced (see example below).

Direct instruction and modeling. Introduce the new grammar skill. Define it and demonstrate how it is used in a sentence. Included here would be examples of the grammar skills as well as nonexamples. ("This is a noun; this is not a noun." "This is a compound sentence; this is not a compound sentence.") Make sure you use "kid language" in your definition and description. This is language that is at the students' level, using words and phrases that are in their listening vocabulary.

Guided practice. Guided practice is where the teacher takes the whole class through the skill and provides support as necessary. Guided practice should enable the student to use the skill independently. It can also be used as a form of "dip-sticking." This is a method to quickly check which students have grasped the skill.

Independent practice. Independent practice invites students to practice or use the skill that has just been taught. If done correctly, students should be able to succeed with a 95 percent success ratio. Ideally, independent practice is done through an authentic writing experience or activity. However, there are times when assignments or activities such as worksheets are appropriate.

Review. Students do not learn any skill in one lesson or setting. With all skills, students need regular practice and review at successively higher levels in order to master it.

Example Grammar Lesson

Presented here is an example of a grammar lesson that uses the elements of effective skills instruction.

I. OBJECTIVE: Students will learn about nouns.
II. DIRECT INSTRUCTION AND MODELING (sometimes called Input).
   1. Today we're going to look at special kinds of words. They are thing words or nouns.
   2. A noun or thing word is something that you can see or feel.

3. It is a thing.
4. These are thing words: bike, car, horse, tree, ball.
   a. You can see all of these.
   b. You could also touch each of these.
   c. They are nouns or thing words.
5. These are other kinds of words that aren't nouns.
   a. They are not nouns because we can't see them.
   b. At, over, slip, happy, in, through, and.

III. GUIDED PRACTICE: Use one of the guided practice activities below.

Activity #1—You show a list of words on the board or poster. (nail, at, this, pen, over, then, bike, in, happy, running, bike, plant, sky, saw, dog). As you read them out loud, students raise their thumbs when they hear a noun or thing word. By watching thumbs you will get a good sense of who's grasped the concept.

Activity #2—Using a worksheet, students do the first two problems together as a class. Then, they do the next three problems with a buddy. You can circulate as students are talking and working here to get a good sense of who's grasped the concept. Finally, have students do two by themselves. Again, circulate to check answers.

IV. INDEPENDENT PRACTICE (sometimes called Activity): Use one of the activities below.

Activity #1—Ask students, "*If you were to take a walk to a favorite place, what are some things you might see? Use your journal to tell us in words and pictures.*" When completed, students read their descriptions out loud in large or small group. Students will see if they can guess where the favorite place might be. This activity has students using the grammar skill indirectly. It is an authentic writing activity and is open-ended so that all students are able to experience success.

Activity #2—If you are using the worksheet for guided practice above, have students complete the worksheet independently. It should be practice of things they've already learned and done. Thus, they should be able to do this with 95 percent to 100 percent success.

Tips for Developing Grammar Awareness

Listed below are seven simple tips for helping students to develop an awareness of grammar in their speaking and writing.

> **Use lots of real writing.** Authentic writing with feedback and response from classmates and teachers is most effective in developing grammar awareness.
>
> **Use worksheets judiciously.** There's nothing wrong with worksheets. They're tools; however, like any tool, their effectiveness is determined by how they're used. Whenever possible, have students work in pairs to complete these. That way they hear the thought processes of others. Remember, the goal is learning and writing, not completing a worksheet and getting a score to record.
>
> **Keep skills instruction brief and quickly paced.** Students need some explicit instruction related to grammar. That is, they need to be told exactly what a noun, or incomplete sentence is (see appendix A for basic grammar rules).
>
> **Use posters and bulletin boards as reminders.**
>
> **Find ways to get students talking about their writing.** Peer group editing is one way to do this.
>
> **Promote voluntary reading.** Wide reading is the cure for almost everything literary.
>
> **Become aware of your own grammar as you are speaking and writing.** Make sure you use correct grammar in your speaking. Correct children's grammatical mistakes without calling a great deal of attention to it. Example:
>
> *"Mr. J, I seen three deer last night."*
>
> *"You mean you saw three deer? How exciting that must have been. Tell me about it."*
>
> In this way you are still honoring the idea while making the quick correction.

Strategies for Developing Grammar Skills

This section contains a description of eight strategies or activities that can be used to enhance students' knowledge of grammar.

Daily Oral Language (DOL)

Daily oral language is a quick, effective way to teach and reinforce grammar and punctuation. Simply write one or two sentences on the board in which there are grammar or punctuation errors. Then ask volunteers to come up and correct an error. Students should correct only one error and then explain why they made their correction. This allows others to hear their thinking and enables you to conduct quick grammar and punctuation mini-lessons. DOL should be kept fairly fast-paced. Eventually, you may include a short paragraph instead of sentences.

Here is an example of five DOL sentences:

1. **bill run fast**
   - Bill ran fast.
   - Bill runs fast.
2. **sara is going with bill to wisconsin**
   - Sara is going with Bill to Wisconsin.
3. **kirsten bob said you know it ain't time for gym class yet**
   - "Kirsten," Bob said, "you know it isn't time for gym class yet."
4. **jim don't know we don't do recess today.**
   - Jim doesn't know we aren't having recess today.
5. **jenny, she lost her new pen**
   - Jenny lost her new pen.

You can find DOL sentences on the Internet (see search terms at the end of this chapter). You could also buy books with lots of DOL sentences in them. However, I've found that it is always more effective to create your own sentences based on the types of errors you see in students' writing and hear in their speaking. Also, create sentences and paragraphs that are about (a) your students, (b) your students' lives or experiences, or (c) books, subjects, themes, or topics you may be studying.

Sentence Combining

Sentence combining is a method of teaching grammar intuitively. In sentence combining, students are given two or more sentences. These sentences may come from a book they're reading, a unit they're studying, current events, or their lives. They must then combine the sentences while keeping the same ideas. The goal is not to make a longer sentence, but rather, to develop more effective sentences. The resulting sentence must be a complete sentence and use as few words as possible. This is a naturalistic approach to grammar as students naturally look for nouns, verbs, propositions, and connecting words to construct new sentences.

Sentence combining invites students to experiment with word choice and order. They begin to realize that there are many ways to build sentence. This provides a more authentic context in which to talk about nouns, verbs, capital letters, and periods. Here are some examples of sentence combining:

- Mickey is a dog.

- He belongs to Andy.

Possible Sentences

- Mickey is a dog that belongs to Andy

- Andy's dog is named Mickey.

- Mickey the dog belongs to Andy.

These are the steps for sentence combining:

1. Write two sentences on the board (or three for more advanced students). The sentences don't have to be related to each other; however, it is helpful if they are related to students' lives, experiences, or something they may be studying in another class.

2. Ask students to combine two sentences into one. They can write their sentence ideas down in a journal or on thinking paper (scratch paper). You can experiment by having students do this orally. They could also do this in pairs or small groups. This enables them to talk and hear the thinking of others. Students should share their ideas with the group or class in some way.

3. Share your own combined sentence or write one student's on the board. Analyze sentences only after students have created them. Identify and discuss the various types of words used and

why. Have a list of possible connecting words someplace on the board or word wall (and, or, unless, because, also). You might identify the thing words (nouns), action words (verbs), and describing words (adjectives). This is a quick and simple way to review the elements that are needed for a complete sentence.

Important note: Always reinforce the notion that a sentence is a complete idea. It needs to make sense by itself. Encourage students to read their sentences out loud to see if they make sense. This can be done quickly by having students turn to a neighbor to share their sentences.

To extend this activity:

4. Ask students to insert words in their sentences to create silly sentences, scary sentences, mysterious sentences, complicated sentences, and so on. This is the type of open-ended activity in which students can participate at their own levels. Encourage more advanced students to include special words or concepts in their sentences.

5. Provide three or more short sentences and ask students to communicate these ideas as effectively and smoothly as they can. They may write two or more sentences or even a paragraph. The goal is smooth effective communication. Again, encourage students to read their sentences out loud to check for accuracy, completion, and fluency of one idea to another. Here is an example of multisentence combining:

- Mickey is a dog.

- He belongs to Andy.

- He is a pug.

- He loves to snuggle.

- He snores when he sleeps.

Possible Sentences

- Andy has a pug named Mickey. Mickey loves to snuggle and he snores when he sleeps.

Sentence Elaboration

In sentence elaboration, students are given a sentence with the direction to make it better or more interesting. This allows students to see the basic structure of a sentence while using propositions, adjectives, verbs, and other types of words and sentence parts to make it more interesting. Creativity and humor should be encouraged. For example, you might ask students to make the sentence more mysterious, funny, efficient, fancy, exciting, boring, scary, loud, bizarre, silly, funny, pig-like, old, new, happy, sad, expensive, and so forth. Again, this is more effective if the original sentence has some connection to what students are reading or studying or from their lives and experiences.

Grammar as Inquiry

Inquiry is when students ask a question and then use data to answer the question. In this case, the question is: How many nouns per hundred (NPH) are in this text? To answer the question, students select a spot in a text or trade book, count out one hundred words, and record the number of nouns to get a NPH score. You can do this with any grammatical element such as verbs per hundred (VPH) or adjectives per hundred (APH). With younger students, use nouns per fifty (NPF).

To extend this activity older students can find three NPH scores in a chapter or text and then calculate the average. Ask an inquiry question in which one type of text is compared to another. For example: Are there more NPH in a newspaper or a Harry Potter book? Which author uses more APH: J. K. Rowling, Kit Pearson, or Jerry Spinelli? These scores can be recorded on a graph and compared. You could also ask the students to notice the type of nouns found in a story. Have them look for different types of nouns, adjectives, or verbs (below). Examples might include floating nouns, nouns that sink, big nouns, little nouns, nouns that bounce, healthy nouns, and so on.

ANIMAL NOUNS   HUMAN NOUNS   NONHUMAN NOUNS

Word Sort

Ask students to identify a specific number of a certain type of words. For example, list thirty verbs found in a particular story. Then, have students examine the group and arrange the verbs (or some other type of word) into groups or categories (figure 23.1). A table or bar graph can be used to record the results. This would enable you to compare the types of verbs found in different stories. (Make sure you use the same number of verbs from each story.)

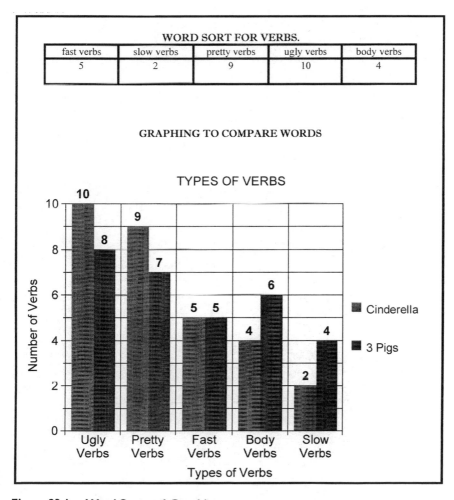

WORD SORT FOR VERBS.

fast verbs	slow verbs	pretty verbs	ugly verbs	body verbs
5	2	9	10	4

GRAPHING TO COMPARE WORDS

Figure 23.1. Word Sort and Graphing

Grammar Treasure Hunt

Ask students to go on a grammar treasure hunt to find various grammatical elements. Using a book or textbook in which they are familiar, students use a graphic organizer to collect and organize data. Tally marks are then used to keep track of how many words are put in each category (see figure 23.2).

Peer Editing

Peer editing (described in chapter 19) can also be used for developing grammar skills. Here you would identify three to five specific grammatical elements upon which to focus (see below).

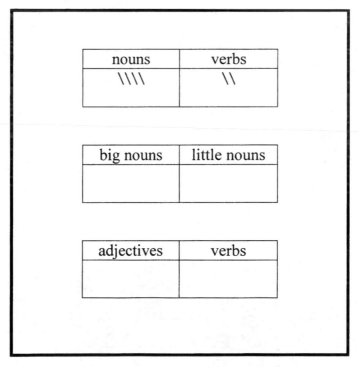

Figure 23.2. Examples of Graphic Organizers for Grammar Treasure Hunt

Editing Checklist

1. Maintains consistent verb tense (past, present, future). yes_____ no _____

2. Compound sentences make sense when pulled apart. yes_____ no _____

3. Sentences are one complete idea. yes_____ no _____

4. Uses "don't" and "doesn't" correctly. yes_____ no _____

5. Uses him/her, she/he/me correctly. yes_____ no _____

Wide Reading

Okay, so this isn't a specific strategy. But voluntary, self-selected, enjoyable reading is the cure for almost everything. Wide reading provides students with an implicit sense of the structure of the language.

Internet Search Terms

Daily oral language: *daily-oral-language, daily-oral-language-activities, daily-oral-language-grammar.*

Grammar activities: *grammar-activities, grammar-lessons, grammar-best-practice, grammar-teaching-strategies, grammar-games, grammar-classroom-games.*

Sentence combining: *grammar-sentence-combining, sentence-combining, sentence-combining activities, sentence-combining-strategies, teaching-tips-sentence-combining.*

Grammar instruction: *grammar-instruction, grammar-instruction-best-practice, grammar-instruction-activities, grammar-instruction-research.*

References

Hillocks, G. (1986) *Research on written composition*. Urbana, Ill.: ERIC Clearing House on Reading and Communication Skills.

Hillocks, G., & Mavrognes, N. (1986) Sentence combining. In Hillocks, G. (Ed.), *Research on Written Composition: New Directions for Teaching* (142–46). Urbana, Ill.: NCTE.

Johnson, A., & Graves, M. (1997) Scaffolding: A tool for enhancing the reading experiences of all students. *Texas Journal of Reading, 3*, 31–37.

Pressley, M., Harris, K. R., & Marks, M. B. (1992) But good skill users are constructivists! *Educational Psychology Review, 4*, 3–31.

GRAMMAR AND PUNCTUATION BRUSH-UP

G rammar is the study of the way language works, a description of the structure of our language. Correct grammar usage helps to create precision in writing and speaking. While you do not have to be a grammarian to write well, you do have to learn a few basic grammar rules and develop an intuitive sound for the language. This chapter describes seven grammar tips and a couple of punctuation tidbits that should get students through most academic writing situations (Johnson, 2003).

There are two ways for students to check their writing for grammar errors: First, have other people read their work. Second, have them use the grammar check programs that come with most word processor programs. While not always reliable, grammar checks can find many grammar mistakes, and they provide students with short grammar lessons as they use them.

Avoiding the Seven Most Common Grammar Errors

1. **Stay consistent with tense.** You may not switch tense on a whim. If you use the past tense in the first part of a sentence or paragraph, you must use it throughout.

> *Incorrect:* After William hit the ball he ran. He stumbles on the way to first (past tense and present tense).

> *Correct:* After William hit the ball he ran. He stumbled on the way to first (both use past tense).

Correct: William hits the ball and runs. He stumbles on the way to first base (both use present tense).

Incorrect: The accident happened because people drive too fast (past and present tense).

Correct: The accident happened because people were driving too fast (past tense).

Correct: Accidents happen because people drive too fast (present tense).

Incorrect: Carlos is dirty because he was (past) out working and his dog keeps (present) knocking him down.

Correct: Carlos is dirty because his dog keeps knocking him down when he is working.

Correct: Carlos is dirty because he was out working and his dog kept knocking him down.

2. **Stay consistent with plurality.** You also may not switch plurality on a whim. If you use the singular in the first part of a sentence or paragraph, you must use it throughout.

Incorrect: A person (singular) should always have their (plural) notebooks.

Correct: A person should always have a notebook.

Correct: People should always have their notebooks.

Incorrect: The class (singular) improved their (plural) scores by 30 percent.

Correct: The class improved its score by 30 percent.

Correct: People in the class improved their scores by 30 percent.

Incorrect: A child (singular) should be allowed to remove their (plural) shoes.

Correct: Children should be allowed to remove their shoes.

Correct: A child should be allowed to remove his or her shoes.

Incorrect: A child (singular) often worries about their (plural) first day of school.

Correct: Children often worry about their first day of school.

Correct: A child often worries about the first day of school.

3. **Double pronouns should make sense when one is missing.** This means that if you read the sentence with just one of either pronouns, that sentence should still make sense.

Incorrect: Me and her will go to the dance. (Me will go to the dance. Her will go to the dance.)

Correct: She and I will go to the dance. (She will go to the dance. I will go to the dance.)

Incorrect: Kelli and her discussed the plan. (Kelli discussed the plan. Her discussed the plan.)

Correct: Kelli and she discussed the plan. (Kelli discussed the plan. She discussed the plan.)

Incorrect: The prize went to he and I. (The prize went to he. The prize went to I.)

Correct: The prize went to him and me. (The prize went to him. The prize went to me.)

Incorrect: Him and me went to the movie. (Him went to the movie. Me went to the movie.)

Incorrect: Him and I went to the movie. (Him went to the movie. I went to the movie.)

Correct: He and I went to the movie. (He went to the movie. I went to the movie.)

4. **Stay gender neutral.**

Incorrect: Every person has to make his own decision.

Correct: Every person has to make his or her own decision.

Best: People have to make their own decisions.

Incorrect: Firemen work long and hard.

Correct: Firefighters work long and hard.

Incorrect: This lake is man-made.

Correct: This lake is made by humans.

Correct: This lake is human-made.

5. **Avoid repetition within a sentence.** By trying to use as few words as possible you will avoid most problems with repetition and redundancy.

Incorrect: Steve often comes to school tired so we must try to get Steve to bed on time.

Correct: Steve often comes to school tired. We must try to get him to bed on time.

Correct: Steve often comes to school tired; therefore, we must try to get him to bed on time.

6. **Use *that* for restrictive clauses and *which* for nonrestrictive clauses.** A restrictive clause is one in which the clause or point is essential to the meaning of the sentence. Use *that* in these instances.

Example: The class that used Andy's book produced excellent writers.

The sentence above indicates that there was a class that used Andy's book and there was also at least one other class that did not. The class that used Andy's book produced excellent writers. Thus, the clause is essential to the point of the sentence as we are clearly identifying a particular class.

A nonrestrictive clause is like a theatrical aside. It adds dimension to the idea; however, the meaning is still largely intact if the clause were not there. Use *which* in these instances.

Example: The class, *which used Andy's book,* produced excellent writers.

In the sentence above, the main idea is that the class produced excellent writers. They just happened to have used Andy's book. It does not indicate that there was another class.

7. **Use *that* for restrictive clauses and *who* for nonrestrictive clauses.**

Restrictive clause: Those students that are done with their work may go to recess.

Nonrestrictive clause: Those students, who are done with their work, may go to recess.

The first one indicates that only those students finished with their work are to be allowed to go recess. The second one indicates that these students are allowed to go to recess and also, they just happen to be done with their work.

Punctuation

This section describes the punctuation information necessary to get you through the majority of students' writing projects.

The Comma

A comma is used in the following situations:

1. **Between elements.** Use a comma to separate items in a series. A comma should be used before the last *and* or *or* in the sentence.

Incorrect: The apples oranges and bananas fell to the ground.

Incorrect: The apples, oranges and bananas fell to the ground.

Correct: The apples, oranges, and bananas fell to the ground.

2. **To separate a nonessential clause.** A nonessential clause, like the nonrestrictive clause described above, is like a theatrical aside. Here, the message is still intact without its inclusion.

Nonessential clause: The orange, which had been handled by George, fell to the ground.

The sentence above indicates that an orange fell to the floor and it just happened to have been handled by George. This is an example of a nonessential clause. The George part of the sentence is an interesting but not essential part of this sentence.

An essential clause means that the information in the middle of the sentence is vital to the stuff at the end and should not be separated by a comma. In the sentence below, there was more than one orange, but only the one handled by George fell to the floor. This is an essential clause; thus, *that* is used instead of *which.*

251

Essential clause: The orange that had been handled by George fell to the floor.

3. To separate two independent clauses joined by a conjunction. If you have a compound sentence where both sides of the sentence would be complete sentences by themselves, use a comma.

Two independent clauses: Apples are better than oranges, and bananas are often used for pie.

Both parts of this sentence above would work as sentences by themselves: Apples are better than oranges. Bananas are often used for pie. A comma is used here to separate them. In the sentence below, a comma is not used. "Apples are better than oranges" is a complete sentence; however, "they are often used for pie" depends on the first part of the sentence for it to make sense, thus, it is a dependent clause.

A compound sentence with one dependent clause: Apples are better than oranges and they are often used for pie.

Do not use a comma to separate two parts of a compound sentence.

Incorrect: Margaret Hamilton played the Wicked Witch, and later starred in coffee commercials.

Correct: Margaret Hamilton played the Wicked Witch and later starred in coffee commercials.

The Semicolon

A semicolon is used in the following situations:

1. To separate two independent clauses that are not joined by a conjunction. This means the semicolon takes the place of *and, but,* and *or.*

No semicolon: The winners were happy but the losers were sad.

Semicolon: The winners were happy; the losers were sad.

2. To separate elements in a series that already contain commas. If I wanted to list a series of things in different groups (some fruit things, some vegetable things, and some dairy things), I would use the commas to separate the things within the groups and semicolons to separate the groups. This way the reader knows when the groups end and begin.

Incorrect: For breakfast there were apples, oranges, and pears, carrots, peas, and beans, and yogurt, cottage cheese, and milk.

Correct: For breakfast there were apples, oranges, and pears; carrots, peas, and beans; and yogurt, cottage cheese, and milk.

The Colon

The rule of thumb for the colon is that everything that follows the colon should directly relate to what preceded it. This is done in two ways:

1. A complete introductory clause followed by a final clause to illustrate the point.

Example: There were three kinds of fruit: apples, oranges, and pears.

2. A complete introductory clause followed by a complete sentence that illustrates the point.

Example: All three agree: Fruit is best for breakfast.

The illustrating sentence that follows the colon above is a complete sentence; thus, it begins with a capital letter.

Final Thoughts

The information included above should get students through most writing situations. If you have any further questions, I would refer you to *A Short Guide to Academic Writing* (2003).

References

Johnson, A. (2003). *A short guide to academic writing.* Lanham, Md.: University Press of America.

ASSESSING GROWTH IN READING

The monthly reading description chart is a way to keep track of students' literacy growth in a positive (some would say sane) manner. Simply create a manila folder containing all or some of the information below. Students would be in charge of keeping track of their own growth here.

Monthly Reading Description Chart
Interesting topics, subjects, or ideas read about:
1.
2.
3.
4.
5.

Books Read	Date Completed
1.	1.
2.	2.
3.	3.
4.	4.
5.	5.
6.	6.
7.	7.
8.	8.

Figure B.1.   Books Read

Skills I use to help me comprehend information books:		
Pre-Reading Comprehension Skills	**During-Reading Comprehension Skills**	**Post-Reading Comprehension Skills**
__ Preview and Overview. __ Web and Brainstorm. __ Outlines and Brainstorm __ Other (describe below)	__ Paragraph Re-Read. __ Read and Pause. __ Other (describe below)	__ Article Re-Read. __ Webbing and Outlining. __ Other (describe below)

Figure B.2.   Comprehension Skills

Describe an interesting character from a book you've read:

Number of book talks _____

Number of book reviews _____

What books or kinds of books would you like to read next month?

What are your reading goals for next month?

Genre or Types of Books Read		
___ fantasy ___ picture book ___ realistic fiction ___ detective/mystery	___ science fiction ___ historical fiction ___ fairy tales ___ adventure	___ fantasy ___ historical ___ information book ___ biography ___ horror/scary book

Figure B.3.   Books Read—Genre

Other skills or strategies used to understand information books:

Skills I use to help me recognize words:
1.
2.
3.
4.

Words per minute scores:

____WPM

____WPM

____WPM

____WPM

New or interesting words:

1.

2.

3.

4.

5.

ACTIVITIES TO DEVELOP PHONEMIC AWARENESS

This appendix contains activities that can be used to develop phonemic awareness. Phonemic awareness is an important prereading skill. These activities are usually used in preschool, kindergarten, and first grade; however, you may find occasion to use them with some older students.

Phonemes

Phoneme.   Phonemes are the smallest units of sound that change the meanings of spoken words. English has about forty-one to forty-four phonemes. A few words, such as *a* or *oh*, have only one phoneme. Most words have more.

Phonemic awareness.   This is the ability to notice, think about, and work with the individual sounds in spoken words. Example: students are aware of or able to combine separate sounds of a word to say the word (/c/ /a/ /t/ = cat).

Activities for Developing Phonemic Awareness

Phoneme addition activity.   Children make a new word by adding a phoneme to an existing word. (Teacher: What word do you have if you add /s/ to the beginning of park? Children: spark.)

Phoneme blending activity.   Children learn to listen to a sequence of separately spoken phonemes, and then combine the phonemes to form a word. (Teacher: What word is /b/ /i/ /g/? Children: /b/ /i/ /g/ is big.)

Phoneme categorization activity.   Children recognize the word in a set of three or four words that has the "odd" sound. (Teacher: Which word doesn't belong? bun, bus, rug. Children: Rug does not belong. It doesn't begin with a /b/.)

Phoneme deletion activity.   Children learn to recognize the word that remains when a phoneme is removed from another word. (Teacher: What is smile without the /s/? Children: Smile without the /s/ is mile.)

Phoneme identity activity.   Children learn to recognize the same sounds in different words. (Teacher: What sound is the same in fix, fall, and fun? Children: The first sound, /f/, is the same.)

Phoneme isolation activity.   Children learn to recognize and identify individual sounds in a word. (Teacher: What is the first sound in van? Children: The first sound in van is /v/.)

Phoneme segmentation activity.   Children break a word into its separate sounds, saying each sound as they tap out or count it. (Teacher: How many sounds are in grab? Children: /g/ /r/ /a/ /b/. Four sounds.)

Phoneme substitution activity.   Children substitute one phoneme for another to make a new word. (Teacher: The word is bug. Change /g/ to /n/. What's the new word? Children: bun.)